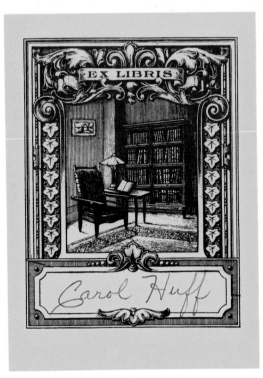

PROMINENT AMERICAN GHOSTS

SUSY SMITH

PROMINENT AMERICAN
GHOSTS

THE WORLD PUBLISHING COMPANY

CLEVELAND AND NEW YORK

Published by The World Publishing Company
2231 West 110th Street, Cleveland, Ohio 44102

Published simultaneously in Canada by
Nelson, Foster & Scott Ltd.

Printed in the United States of America.

CONTENTS

PREFACE

WHAT IS A GHOST? Is it the spirit of a deceased person, who still actually lives in some other sphere of existence, and is occasionally able to manifest itself to certain individuals on earth? Some ghosts look and act as if they may be those whom they purport to be, still able to think and perform with purpose. They appear for a definite reason—perhaps to give information about something that they had left undone during their lives, or to warn loved relatives of impending danger.

A friend of mine and her daughter were once driving down a Florida country road at night when they saw my friend's late husband standing in front of them, holding up his hand for them to stop. He was clearly identifiable in the car lights, but when they got out and went to the spot where he had been seen, he had disappeared. They then walked ahead on the road a short distance and discovered that around the next bend a bridge was washed out. They are sure they would have been killed had they not been stopped.

One night when actor James Cagney was speeding down a California highway, he and his wife both heard the voice of his deceased father telling him to slow down. Heeding the warning the second time it occurred, they soon came upon a wrecked trailer in the middle of the highway, into which they undoubtedly would have crashed at the higher rate of speed.

Ghosts have been known to give evidence of their identity to strangers. An Englishman on his first night in a new, family-style hotel was visited by the apparition of a young gentleman in tennis clothes, who glared at him as if he were an intruder. Upon investigation the next morning, the man learned that a former roomer, a tennis enthusiast, had recently died in his bed. When he was shown a group photograph, the Englishman pointed out his spectral visitor, who was indeed the previous occupant of his room.

Some ghosts appear in order to bring information of their own deaths. American playwright and theatrical producer David Belasco issued a booklet with the same title as his highly popular play *The Return of Peter Grimm,* in which he wrote:

> My mother convinced me that the dead come back by coming to me at the time of her death. One night . . . I was awakened . . . and was then greatly startled to see my dear mother (whom I knew to be in San Francisco) standing close by me. As I strove to speak and to sit up she smiled at me a loving, reassuring smile, and spoke my name—the name she called me in my boyhood—"Davy, Davy, Davy." Leaning down she seemed to kiss me, then drew away a little and said, "Do not grieve. All is well and I am happy!" then moved toward the door and vanished. The next day I related the incident to my family and expressed the conviction that my mother was dead.

Later that day Belasco received a telegram to the effect that his mother had died during the night, shortly before the time he had seen her.

Other ghosts, rather than giving evidence of being the actual individuals returning, seem to be mere shades or memories of the deceased persons. Appearing occasionally at the places where they were happiest, or unhappiest, or at the scene of a great crime in which they participated, they are more like a picture, somehow left indelibly in the atmosphere at that particular site. This type of haunting has been characterized by psychical researcher Frederic W. H. Myers as a "veridical afterimage"—a memory impression left by the individual when he was alive and under some great emotional stress. Numerous famous apparitions in old houses answer this description.

Ghosts have also been explained as idea-patterns—a mental moving picture in three dimensions, created by the dramatic cooperation of the unconscious minds of the appearer and of those who see his apparition. This concept presupposes that the spirit of the appearer is still living somewhere, in some form, and that his mind is still active and able to impress the minds of others.

There are those who will tell you that an apparition is actually originated by the person who sees it—a hallucination that is the result of an expectation to see a ghost, nerves, alcohol, or too much pizza. It is more often a person who has not seen a ghost who says this. One who has had the actual experience is usually convinced of the phenomenon's existence external to and completely independent of himself.

The condition, whatever it is, which makes for ghostliness does not often prevail. And when it does, there are only certain people who are able to be aware of it. This, it is claimed, is because they are more "psychic" or "sensitive" than others—they are tuned in to the proper wavelength. Not everyone can see an apparition even when others in the room with him are observing it. Certain individuals may see and hear it; others may experience it visually but not auditorily; still others may hear it speak but not be able to see it; and at least one insensitive soul will sit there during the entire time, wondering why everyone else is so strangely gaping and gasping, and perhaps even shivering and shaking. Completely unable to experience a thing out of the ordinary, this last person will state emphatically that ghosts are bosh and humbug, and that he is the only sane man in the place.

A quiet, almost shy wraith, known as "The Dark Lady of Bognor" or "The Morton Ghost" because pseudonyms were used when the case was first published in the *Proceedings* of the Society for Psychical Research, appeared from time to time over a period of years. Her sphere of action has since been identified as Garden Reach House, Cheltenham, England. One of the family living there from 1882–1889, the years when the ghost was seen, was Miss Rose Despard, considered to be capable of objective inquiry because she was a medical student at the time. She kept careful records, supplemented by signed statements from six witnesses, of the apparition's every appearance, noting who saw her, where she walked, and where she stood. All the members of the family observed the lady at one time or another except the father, who was never able to see her even when she was in plain sight of everyone else in the room.

Perhaps there is no one explanation that covers all manifestations of a ghostly nature. Maybe there are several different causes, depending upon varying conditions. But no matter what the reason, there is one thing that can truly be said about ghosts: They do appear—to a great many people, in a great many places. They are not old wives' tales, or superstition, or trickery. And they have brought true information too many times to be attributable merely to imagination, or mass hallucination, or even mass hypnosis. Whatever they are—ghosts are real!

England is usually thought of as having the most haunts because it has so many old castles and houses, where they are a cherished family heritage. It might surprise many Americans, therefore, to learn that countless old homes in this country also have authentic ghosts. People, as well as houses, may be haunted on occasion by the exciting "poltergeists." It must be said, however, that the traditional frightening story-tale spook of clanking chains and ghoulish groans is almost entirely fictional.

Ghosts have become famous in a number of American communities either because they are alleged to be the returning spirits of local heroes or because they have existed for so long that they have become legendary traditions. On occasion they have gained national renown by being written up in books, magazines, and newspapers. While doing research on these well-known entities for *Prominent American Ghosts,* I have traveled widely throughout the United States, visiting many charming old homes from coast to coast, and in Hawaii, and meeting many interesting people.

I think I also met a few of the ghosts—but I'm not sure.

PROMINENT AMERICAN GHOSTS

CHAPTER ONE

THE LATE
MRS. NELLY BUTLER

AT THE TOPMOST TIP OF MAINE the first American highway begins. Highway 1 continues down the northeast side of the state until it reaches the sea, and there it soon comes to the town of Machias— pronounced Ma-*chy*-as—and its nearby village of Machiasport. It was right in this area that the first recorded American ghost appeared. Nelly Butler was not, of course, the earliest phantom in this country; but she was the first to be written up and substantiated with sworn testimonies. This is what makes her truly unique—that over one hundred observers declared themselves to have either seen or heard her. Perhaps the most significant of all her "firsts" is that she was witnessed by more people than any other ghost, before or since.

It was on the night of August 9, 1799, in the house of Mr. Abner Blaisdel, on the coast near Machiasport, that a disembodied voice was heard announcing that its owner was going to appear in the village. Abner Blaisdel was a man of piety and upright character, and he wished to retain that reputation; so the members of his family were told to keep to themselves the story of this strange voice from out of nowhere. They well knew the ridicule with which such a tale would be met by their practical, God-fearing, seafaring neighbors.

As time passed and the sound did not come again, the Blaisdels finally decided that they had let themselves be fooled by the whispering wind, and they forgot about the whole affair. But five months later, on January 2, 1800, the voice was heard again in the house. It was obviously a woman speaking, and she told her listeners she was Captain George Butler's deceased wife, who, they well knew, had been David Hooper's daughter Nelly. She ordered them to send two messengers straightaway to fetch her father.

The disembodied voice had a very authoritative sound. No one dared refuse to do its bidding, so David Hooper was sent for. Wondering, ridiculing, and grumbling at the foolishness, the old man made the six-mile trip. But when he heard the very tone and manner of his daughter's voice speaking to him, he became convinced that he was actually listening to her departed spirit. When he wrote his affidavit about this and subsequent experiences, he stated that she gave "such clear and irresistible tokens of her being the spirit of my own daughter as gave me no less satisfaction than admiration and delight."

The admiration and delight were never to come to the Blaisdels, however. They always felt very put upon at being the chosen subjects for the visitations. Nelly Butler even made her first appearance to one of them—Captain Paul Blaisdel, Abner's son. Captain Paul was walking through a field one day in late January 1800, when he saw an "unreal-looking" figure of a woman in the distance. In a few moments she had moved rapidly toward him. She had never touched the ground, he said in his affidavit, but had seemed to float just above it. Her raiment, he said, was "as white as possible." He was literally dumbfounded by the apparition, and could say nothing to it before it vanished.

The next evening "the Spectre," as Nelly was afterward called, appeared at Abner's house again, and rebuked Paul for not speaking to her, an old friend and neighbor, in the field. After this visitation, to the vast relief of the family, there was a respite from her attentions. In March, however, Mrs. Butler returned and chatted for two hours with the four Blaisdels, whom she insisted must go down into the cellar for the interview. It was frightening to be sitting in the dark cellar talking to an invisible entity, but no one had the nerve to resist her demands. She told them that "though my body is consumed and turned to dust, my soul is as much alive as before I left the body." She always spoke in religious terms, and usually began with many "Hallelujahs." One might almost suspect that Nelly had the soul of an evangelist, and was enjoying her revival in more ways than one.

A whole month passed before she came again; but in May she was back for six one-night stands. From then on the entire countryside was agog with gossip, innuendo, and questions. Was she or wasn't she the deceased spirit she claimed to be? And if not, *what* was she?

By now her manifestations had become visible to some people, although others still only heard her. Among the latter, some heard her words distinctly; a few heard a strange voice but could not understand the words spoken. Some persons who were unable at first to see the Spectre succeeded in doing so after repeated visits. A few poor unfavored individuals could neither see nor hear her, and they quite naturally suspected their neighbors' sanity. Yet of those who testified as to the evidence they had received of her existence, most could both see and hear her, and she was usually in a shining white garment. All to whom she appeared agreed that the form and features were those of the deceased woman she claimed to be, and they all testified to the bright light which came from her, so that it illumined a field at night and shone like a lamp in the cellar.

A typical description of the order of events at these seances was given by a stranger to the district, Mary Gordon, who came to Machiasport out of great curiosity. Mary stayed at the Blaisdel home on the night of August 4. (Apparently this poor family had to keep open house all the time, for if they turned anybody away it would have been claimed that they did not want their fraud to be detected.) Mary Gordon said that about two hours before daylight there was a barrage of loud knocks that awakened everybody. It was the regular procedure of the ghost to announce her coming by a series of knocks, and so, hastily dressing, Mary went downstairs. There she joined the rest of the assembly—most of whom must have slept on the floor, for they numbered about twenty —and they all trooped down into the cellar, which by this time was known to be the Spectre's favorite spot. "Then," writes Mary, "I heard such a voice speaking to us as I never heard before nor since. It was shrill but mild and pleasant.

"Mr. Blaisdel, in addressing the voice, said that several persons (of whom I was one) had come from a distance to obtain satisfaction, and desired that she would tell us who she was, and the design of her coming. She answered, 'I was once N.H. and after I was married, I was N.B.' After much conversation upon the design of her coming, she appeared to us. At first the apparition was a mere mass of light: then grew into personal form, about as tall as myself. We stood in two ranks about four or five feet apart.

Between these ranks she slowly passed and repassed, so that any of us could have handled her. When she passed by me, her nearness was that of contact; so that if there had been a substance, I should have certainly felt it. The glow of the apparition had a constant tremulous motion. At last the personal form became shapeless—expanded every way, and then vanished in a moment."

Everyone at the Blaisdels' was at first so frightened of the Spectre that the children had moved their beds into their parents' room. Nelly did not like to be an object of fear, and that may be why she usually held her meetings in the cellar—away from the family rooms. A medium would say that the cellar made an excellent seance room because the "power to manifest" could be built up more strongly in a confined dark space. Whatever her reasons, Mrs. Butler tried to pacify the Blaisdel children. She said, "Be not afraid—you need not be. I never hurt you, did I? And I shall not hurt you now. Put your things in place." And so the children took her at her word and moved back into their own rooms; and, it is true, she never did anything to harm them.

In the area at this time lived a most deserving minister, Abraham Cummings. He was a well-educated man, a graduate of Brown University, but he was also unworldly enough never to worry about food, shelter, or raiment. Apparently his faith was justified, because in 1793, when he had been a supply pastor for a Congregational Church in Bath, Maine, his parishioners had presented him with a sailboat. From then on he conducted most of his ministry from this boat, cruising along the coast and going ashore to preach in the small settlements among the islands and on the mainland. When he reached Machias he heard about the famous Spectre, and he was shocked—badly shocked. Though his congregations were simple folk, he had certainly thought they were of a higher intellectual level than to take such ungodly supernatural stories seriously. He contemplated giving them a resounding sermon on the fallacies of blind superstition.

During June, while he was in Machiasport, there were no reports of visits from the Spectre, and the Reverend Mr. Cummings credited his presence with keeping the irrational element of his flock in line. Then one evening in July, some excited people ran to him saying that the Spectre had returned. What should he do about it? he wondered. He paced the floor for a time, trying to decide how best to cope with the situation. Finally his curiosity got the better of him; he left his home and walked out to see for himself.

Crossing the open field in front of his house, the preacher noticed a slight knoll or rise in the ground about two hundred feet ahead of him. There he could see a group of white rocks on the slope, showing dimly against the dark turf. "Probably something such as that is all the ghost amounts to," he thought, as he kept walking toward the knoll. But when he looked up two or three minutes later, his jaw dropped perceptibly. One of those white rocks had risen off the ground and was now taking the shape of a globe of light with a rosy tinge. He turned directly toward the amazing spectacle so that he could examine it closely. As he walked forward he kept his eyes fixed on this light, for fear it might disappear, but he had not gone more than five paces when the glowing mass flashed right to where he was. Instantly the light resolved itself into the shape of a woman. Her size was abnormally small, however, perhaps that of a child of seven. Staring at her in amazement, the parson thought, "You're not tall enough for the woman who has been appearing among us." Immediately, the figure expanded to normal size, and, he wrote afterward, "she appeared glorious," with rays of light shining from her head like a halo extending clear to the ground.

Cummings, not being conversant with the etiquette of ghostly circles, just stared. He seemed to remember having read somewhere that if one ever met an apparition he must let it speak first, so he politely kept silent. All the while, as he gazed at the vision, he was filled with two strangely conflicting emotions. One, he says, was genuine fright. "But," he adds in his account of his experience, "my fear was connected with ineffable pleasure."

In another moment the Spectre was gone, but the influence of that radiant apparition never left the Reverend Mr. Cummings for the rest of his life. After that, he says, all mundane things seemed dull and commonplace and of no real value. Gone now was his amused contempt for the ignorant yokels who had been taken in by ghost stories. He had seen for himself. He believed. And he was the kind of man who would try to do something about it. From that time forward he investigated every instance of the Spectre's appearance about which he heard, and talked with every witness. He it was who later published the account of all the strange happenings, accompanied by the testimony of every beholder he could contact.

An edition of his pamphlet that is still in existence—a copy of it is at Brown University—was published in Bath in 1826, the year before Abraham Cummings' death. Another edition was issued in Portland in 1859, and of it there are three copies extant. Unfortunately, Cummings told his story very badly in these pamphlets. He may have been brilliant in the pulpit, but on paper he is tedious and dull, wasting many pages in theological argument to prove that ghostly communicants are not contrary to Holy Writ. Cummings was no journalist; he tantalized rather than reported, managing, when he finally got to the plot of his story, to leave out even such an important detail as the location of the events. He supposed that everyone *knew* where it had happened. (After all, by the time Cummings wrote up the case, the Spectre had been the *cause célèbre* of the Maine coast for twenty-six years.) It is only incidentally that one learns the full names of the main characters in Cummings' pamphlet—you have to figure out from the affidavits, for instance, which Blaisdel was Nelly's host. Everyone testifying to the apparition was extremely reluctant to mention first names. Even the ghost is called "N. Butler," or "N.B.," all the way through, and it is only Mary Bragdon, the next to last witness in the book, who states that "the Spirit told us she was once Nelly Butler."

Abraham Cummings said his desire was "to present to the public a complete, satisfactory analysis of this whole mystery"—and he does anything else but that. Still, his motives were good. His effort was made primarily because of the unfortunate charges that had been laid against the Blaisdels; and he wished his evidence to exonerate them of the persistent implications of fraud, which arose largely from the fact that the Spectre had given orders for her husband, Captain George Butler, to marry one of Abner Blaisdel's daughters, Lydia.

Lydia and George had been eying one another favorably for some time previously, and maybe Nelly thought she would help a good cause along. Which just goes to show that death does not give one infallibility, or perhaps that even a ghostly finger in the pie can be one too many. Abner Blaisdel was determined that the match should not take place; and, as soon as the Spectre started pushing it, so was Lydia.

"No, sir," she protested indignantly, if tearfully, "I will not do it."

"Why not?" asked Captain Butler, with a man's innocence in such matters.

"I will not marry a man who has been scared into proposing by a ghost, and that's all there is to it." Lydia was adamant—at the time.

Captain Butler was not at first too insistent. He could hardly have been eager to indulge in the intimacies of the bedchamber with a new wife while his old wife was still so obviously hovering about—and so interested in his affairs. And yet, why should he let a former spouse's espousal of his cause keep him from his happiness? And so at length, as Cummings says, "Capt. Butler's unreserved and honorable confession and his renewed assurances that his *own* will was his, as well as that of his deceased wife, did, with the words of the Spectre, prevail."

When the marriage plans were made public, the gossip started in earnest. Lydia, it was said, was obviously somehow dressing up and appearing as the Spectre, and using a sounding board of some kind to produce the voices—all just in order to get a husband.

The girl gave up. "Worn out by unjust reproaches abroad and these vexations at home," Abraham Cummings writes, "she at last told Capt. Butler, offering him a golden token of her constant affection, that she could bear these miseries no longer, and that they must separate. He pleaded the impropriety of her conduct after such evidence that the appointment was divine. His plea was the waste of words. She dismissed him utterly and forever. This I had by the favor of Capt. Butler himself."

Lydia next tried to sail off in a vessel that had come into port. Bound and determined to get away, she thought she would visit relatives about two hundred miles down the coast; but "the miraculous voice solemnly warned her in the hearing of several witnesses, that her efforts were vain, and that her affliction would sail with her." So once again Captain Butler was sent for, and this time he stubbornly refused to allow anybody, visible or invisible, to mess things up for him. The nuptials were celebrated shortly afterward.

Oddly enough, within twenty-four hours of the wedding, the Spectre came to Captain Butler and whispered, "Be kind to Lydia, for she will not be with you long. She will have one child and die within the year." This came to pass as predicted. Ten months afterward Lydia gave birth to a child and died the next day.

One is inclined to wonder if the first Mrs. Butler's meddling in her husband's affairs might have been more malicious than any-one quite realized, intended to make sure that he would marry someone who would not outlive her in his affections. But perhaps this is to malign a pure spirit.

Nelly knew that from the moment of the wedding the gossip would increase, and it did. On one occasion she told a large crowd of people that on account of her visits to this house the Blaisdel family had been subjected to cruel and wicked gossip and false accusations, and she predicted that these would grow even worse. It must be said that she did make several efforts to clear Lydia of the charges of fraud that she had been responsible for causing. Once, when she had a sizable audience in the Blaisdel cellar, the Spectre ordered Lydia to go upstairs, attended by two women, and sit on the hearth in one of the rooms. Then the star performer carried on triumphantly in the cellar, proving that what she said could not possibly have been the work of Lydia and a sounding board or ventriloquism or anything else.

Another time, she had all the people assembled get up and go for a hike. They marched in a procession at her command, two by two in a solemn step, "as at a funeral," trudging a matter of a couple of miles and back. The wraith herself brought up the end of the procession, marching as the partner of the highly unwill-ing Lydia Butler—who had never yet been able to muster up much affection for her husband's first wife. Much to Lydia's dismay, on this occasion Nelly floated alongside her all the way. This was done apparently for one reason only: that all the people should see Nelly *with* Lydia and know that the two could not possibly, by any trick or fraud, be one.

Even when they saw the phenomenon of her appearance, or heard her voice, some of the people of the community did not believe they were witnessing the actual ghost of Mrs. Butler. They had recourse to only one other theory to explain the apparition, but it seemed logical to them. They believed that this wraith of a dead woman must be a "simulacrum fashioned by the Devil."

This was the position taken by Nelly's sister, Mrs. Sally Went-worth, although her parents were quite convinced to the contrary. The austere Mrs. Wentworth's testimony may be more illuminating of her character and disposition than she realized. She writes: "August 8. I was there with about thirty others and heard much conversation. Her voice was still hoarse and thick, like that of my sister on her deathbed, but more hollow. Sometimes it was clear, and always pleasant. A certain person did, in my opinion very unwisely, ask her whether I was a true Christian. The reply was, 'She thinks she is, she thinks she is. She is my sister.' "

Mrs. Wentworth says she was for a time convinced it was Nelly speaking, especially when a private conversation was reported to her which she and her sister had held and which had never been revealed to another soul. But, she wonders, "Could not some evil spirit hear that conversation, and afterwards personate my sister and reveal it?"

If it was easier for Mrs. Wentworth to believe that an evil spirit could exist and impersonate Nelly than that her own sister could return from the grave, others were more readily convinced that the Spectre's claims were true. Among these was Captain George Butler, who had been satisfied of the ghost's identity almost from the start.

Captain Butler writes:

"When I was called to talk with this voice, I asked, 'Who are you?' It answered, 'I was once your wife.' The voice asked me, 'Do you not remember what I told you when I was alive?' I answered, 'I do not really know what you mean.' The voice said, 'Do you not remember I told you I did not think I should live long with you? I told you that if you were to leave me I should never wish to change my condition; but that if I were to leave you, I could not blame you if you did.'

"This passed between me and my first wife, while she was alive, and there was no living person within hearing, but she and myself, and I am sure that this was never revealed to any person, and no living person could have told it to me before the voice did. As Lydia [Mrs. Butler] and I stood side and side alone [a little distance from the rest of the company], she had her left arm round me and her right hand hold of the forward part of my waistcoat, her head leaning against my breast. There was something appeared to my view right before me, like a person in a winding sheet and her arms folded under the winding sheet, and on her arm there appeared to be a very small child. By this appearance I did not know possibly but I might be deceived. I reached out my left hand to take hold of it. I saw my hand in the middle of it, but could feel nothing. That same evening it appeared and disappeared to me three times."

The testimony of George Butler was corroborated by four other people who said that on that occasion they had seen the same things he had described.

Apparently the reason that Nelly held a baby when she appeared to her husband was because she had died in childbirth, as Lydia was also destined to do. For some strange reason the Spectre insisted upon having her infant's body exhumed and reburied in another spot about thirty feet away. Cummings is at his most nebulous when he states, "There seemed no reason for doing this at the time it was ordered but 18 months later its purpose was understood." He leaves his readers' curiosity forever unsatisfied on this score.

Besides her orders to have certain unaccountable acts performed, the ghost of Mrs. Butler was also famous for her extrasensory perception. She foretold a legal suit involving the Blaisdels, evidently one growing out of the gossip over this affair, and just how it would result. Again, on one of her earliest visits, Abner Blaisdel asked her about his father, who, he had heard, was sick. York, Maine, where his father lived, was two hundred miles away, and news traveled slowly in those days. The Spectre promptly answered that his father was dead. Blaisdel later learned that his father had truly died seven days before.

Nelly was quite a ham, and she enjoyed her role and the notoriety she was receiving. She was always declaiming, besides her "Hallelujahs," such phrases as "I am the voice crying in the wilderness," and "I am from above, praising God and the Lamb." Some of her listeners were surprised, because in life she had never been known for her devoutness. Abner Blaisdel, describing some of her Christian declarations, says, "I then spake to her myself, and said, 'I never knew that you experienced a change of nature before you died, and I should be glad if you would tell when you experienced it.' 'It was,' said she, 'when I laid upon my death bed.' Then she spake to her parents, and reminded them of the conversation which had passed between them at that time, respecting the loss of her child. 'Then it was,' said she, 'that I received my change.'" Her parents joyfully confirmed her statements.

A concluding testimony, chosen from among the dozens quoted

by Cummings, shows how another man who at first completely disbelieved in the phenomenon later wrote of his experience. Mr. Paul Simson, Jr., submits: "August 9, 1800. I was at Mr. A. Blaisdel's with many more, and heard the sound of knocking. It was addressed, and a voice answered, but I could not understand it. Several persons spoke, but received no satisfactory answer. The people generally concluded that the whole affair was some deception. Therefore they went off and I among them. But my reflections on the singular knocking induced me to say to two young men, 'If you will go back, I will, and find out something more if possible; for I am no more satisfied now than I was before I went to that house.' We went back. Mr. Blaisdel asked us why we returned. I told him that we had all gone off with the opinion that the whole affair was a scheme contrived by his daughters, and nothing more, and I meant if possible to find them out.

" 'You must think as you please,' said he, 'I am clear, and I believe my family is.' I told him I wished to see all his family sitting in one part of the room. They complied. Then I took a candle and stood in the midst of the room. After several minutes, something rapped near where two of us stood, and from thence removed to several parts of the house. 'What do you think of it?' said Mr. Blaisdel. 'It appears,' said I, 'to be strange.' 'We will go into the cellar,' said Mr. Blaisdel, 'and if you think anybody is there, search the cellar through with a candle.' We did so. I came out last and was careful and watched, so that I was sure that no person went down. Also the outer door was fast. Then again we heard the sound of knocking. It was addressed, and conversation followed, in the midst of which Mr. Blaisdel said to me, 'If you think any living person talks, go forward and grasp that person.' I went forward a few steps, but was so convinced that nobody was there that I considered all further attempts as useless.

"After much discourse, which I cannot remember, the spirit told us that we must go up and come down again in order, two and two, and she would appear to us. We did so, and I saw the apparition at first about two feet in height; but, as it drew nearer to me, it appeared as tall as a person. I saw this appearance passing *close by me and from me five or six times.* At last it diminished to about a foot in height and then vanished."

Well, what are we to make of all this? Was a whole community suddenly mass-hypnotized? Was the preacher's pamphlet a hoax, and if so why? Certainly Cummings' contemporaries accepted it as an honest tale. And most certainly a few old-timers in that part of Maine still refer to "the Machias ghost" as something that has been handed down to them by tradition. Why don't we just take the whole tale at face value, then?

In that case, the story is simply this: A deceased woman made herself evident to the people of her community for over a year and then disappeared again forever. What possibly could have been her object? Cummings thinks it was "to try to prove the truth of immortality."

Whatever her reasons, we have to admit that this is not only the first recorded ghost story of our country, but also quite the most remarkable.

CHAPTER TWO

THE PATTER
OF LITTLE FEET

THE SOUND OF RUNNING FOOTSTEPS and childish laughter is most pleasant in a house, even if there are no children living there. A ghost whose primary manifestations are of this nature isn't to be shunned by any means. In fact, such an entity should hire out at so much an hour to some of the other gloomy places to be discussed in this book. So no one complains that the old Robert E. Lee mansion in Alexandria, Virginia, is haunted, because its haunts are among the most delightful and inventive ever to be recorded.

Tucked away on Oronoco, a quiet side street, this boyhood home of the great Confederate general is now owned and occupied by investment banker Henry Koch and his family. They didn't know they were buying a haunted house when they acquired this lovely old relic in 1962. Even when they entered the hallway on moving day, June 10, and heard sounds of running and laughter upstairs, they thought it was their son William, who was seven years old at the time. Imagine their surprise, then, to see young Bill appear from a different direction downstairs and assure them that he had been nowhere near the upper hallway. The moving men arrived, and their minds were taken away from the problem; but it returned regularly every day for some time afterward.

Rarely did the sounds occur at night, when even ghostly children should be safely tucked in their beds. But during the day the Kochs became familiar with the little running footsteps and the happy laughter that so often accompanied them.

"It would walk along with us, giggling," Mrs. Koch said. "It sounded as if it were coming from a child about four years old; the laughter was at about the level of our knees." Every member of the family independently heard the sounds frequently. Sometimes the invisible little one would follow them, and sometimes it seemed to circle round and round them as they walked along—particularly in the front hall and up and down the stairway.

"It was so cheery," Mrs. Koch told me, "that we were really disappointed when we stopped hearing it so often." They only hear it once in a while now, but for the first six months they lived in the house the happy laughter rang out sometimes two or three times a day almost every day.

They have, of course, done what they could to attempt to learn where in the history of their home the little one can be placed. The fact that the Robert E. Lees had a child who had been killed falling down stairs at about the age of four years would seem significant were it not that that was long after Lee or any member of his family had ceased to live in this house. The death occurred at the palatial Lee family home at Stratford, Virginia, about fifty miles away.

Because they didn't really want to think that they were suddenly all having some kind of private mental aberration, the Kochs were glad when the milkman asked them one day shortly after they moved in, "Have you heard the little Lees?"

"Yes, we have," Mrs. Koch said, glad to have their secret out in the open for once. But the milkman was already leaving. He had no time for a chat about it.

"Well," he tossed over his shoulder, "if you don't bother them, they won't bother you."

As people so often do, Mrs. Koch neglected to realize the importance of getting the name of the milkman, and by the time she thought of asking him more about what he knew of the "little Lees," he had been transferred to another route.

The Kochs are avid antique collectors, and their home reflects their interest. One of their most prized possessions is a huge ornate gilt mirror bearing the crest of the Lee family which hangs in the downstairs front hall. The three-story red brick house at 607 Oronoco, with its classically simple lines, large high-ceilinged rooms, and beautiful woodwork, has crystal chandeliers from Ireland and gracious fireplaces in the two living rooms. Its crumbling stone front doorsteps reveal their great age, for they were put there in 1790. The back part of the house was built even earlier—in 1770.

The home was originally owned by one John Potts and sold to

Colonel William Fitzhugh, a distant kinsman of Robert E. Lee's mother, Ann Carter Lee. Fitzhugh was one of George Washington's best friends, and the President spent a great deal of time in the house. According to his diaries, he stayed for the night every time he was invited for dinner here. In fact, the last time Washington was entertained before his death was in this house. When the Marquis de Lafayette made a return visit to the United States he was entertained here also.

The history of Robert E. Lee's occupancy of the house begins with the fact that his father, General Henry Lee, had fallen on bad times. The Revolutionary War general, who was known affectionately to his men as "Light Horse Harry" Lee, had been a brilliant, lovable, vigorous man, but somehow after the war he suffered a strange change of mental outlook. The tragedy of his life then began, as he became sensitive, resentful, and imperious, and developed a mania for wild speculation in an effort to make a sudden fortune. Soon he had lost so much money in unprofitable investments that he could not pay his creditors, and he was twice put into jail.

When his son Robert was three years old, the family was forced to leave Stratford, the old ancestral home of the Lees, and William Fitzhugh gave them the Alexandria house to live in. After his experiences in jail, Light Horse Harry Lee had only one desire—to leave the country—and he soon went to Barbados, leaving his wife and three children to fend for themselves on Oronoco Street. The elder Lee stayed away seven years, and died while on his return trip, when Robert was about eleven years old.

Whether from worry and grief or from a physical malady, Robert's mother became an invalid and rarely left her bedroom. The boy had a strong feeling of responsibility, and a need to watch over his mother. A staircase was even built from his bedroom to his mother's, so that he could be available immediately if she needed help. The family lived in this house until Robert was eighteen, when he entered West Point.

Oddly enough, history was to repeat itself in the life of this great man, for aside from the time spent at West Point and in military campaigns, he was nursing women almost continuously. His wife, Mary Custis, Mrs. George Washington's great-great-granddaughter, after presenting Lee with seven children, spent most of the rest of her life an invalid from arthritis.

Another interesting note before we leave Robert E. Lee—after Appomattox he stayed in Alexandria with his cousin, Cassius Lee, who lived at the corner of Oronoco and Washington streets. One day the then current owner of number 607 was startled to look out of the dining room window and see General Lee, who had climbed the fence, wandering around the large and lovely garden. When approached, Lee explained that he felt an urge to see the snowball bushes in bloom for one last time, because he knew he would never be in Alexandria or northern Virginia again. He was right. He never returned, and died a year or two later.

Now, back to the ghostly manifestations observed in the home by the Koch family. The next thing that surprised them occurred when Henry Koch was having a business meeting in the living room downstairs. Floods of music from some kind of stringed instrument suddenly poured forth through the house. Mr. Koch's daughter "Deede," who was eighteen at the time, had a guitar; but her father didn't have any idea she played that well. He gave her the credit, anyway, saying, "That must be my daughter Deede." All the men at the meeting listened to the music and commented about it. Later, her father complimented Deede on her beautiful music, only to learn that she had not been playing—in fact, her guitar had been left at school.

Mrs. Koch also heard a few bars of stringed music one day, and she could not identify the instrument either. It stopped as suddenly as it started.

One day Mrs. Koch lost her cigarette lighter, and looked everywhere for it. All at once, as she was walking out of the living room into the dining room, the lighter came flying from somewhere and landed on the floor at her feet. No one was anywhere around in front of her, and Deede and Henry were together in the living room back of her.

When incidents like the last few are reported, one is tempted to ask, "And where was Bill?" Young boys in haunted houses are often suspected of throwing things, or of secretly producing phenomena and then denying it. And they have sometimes been found to be guilty. But Bill, according to his mother, was always carefully accounted for at times like these. In fact, "Where's Bill?" was probably the first thing that popped into any of their minds.

Sometimes the doorbell of this house rings; but when Mrs. Koch answers it, there is nobody there. She has learned to hurry, too;

in case a neighborhood youngster is playing pranks, she wants to catch him at it. Then again, she does not rule out the possibility that General Washington, or Lafayette, might be coming to call. In that house, who would be surprised at anything?

Twice, friends of the Kochs have said to them, "Do you know this house is haunted?" In both cases they were English people visiting in this country, who could have had no logical way to know the house's secret. I myself had an interesting experience there. Being psychically sensitive, when I walked into the back part of the downstairs hall under the landing, I got a prickly sensation along my spine. It was not a scary feeling—actually it was more like the delicious chills you get when someone kisses your ear or the back of your neck. When I mentioned that the back hall gave me pleasant goose bumps, I was told that this was the spot where the English visitors had also noticed something unusual.

A very curious phenomenon—whether caused by ghosts, poltergeists, optical illusions, or what, no one knows—occurred one Sunday noon when some neighbors, a retired admiral and his wife, were invited over for a visit. Drinks were served, but nobody had had more than one. As the lady guest was sitting there talking, suddenly she was in the midst of a snowstorm. She looked as if she were inside one of those little glass balls that you shake to produce a snowstorm. The rest of the group just stared at her, for the approximately two minutes it lasted, and she went on talking as if she hadn't noticed.

It's a cute scene, really. The gracious host and hostess sitting quietly, but inwardly all a-twitter, never daring to mention what they see for fear that their guest may have brought with her some strange anomaly. The guest, on her part, enduring the curious experience in silence, rather than calling attention to something that may have gone wrong in her hosts' home. However, enough is enough, even of good manners. When, about five minutes later, the big white flakes again began dropping from the air above the admiral's wife, she said pleasantly, "Henry, what do you suppose this is all around me?"

Once it came out into the open—or rather, into the conversational pool—everyone gabbled at once, suggesting this and that, trying to comprehend what actually was happening. They could plainly see the snow coming down, from about a foot above the woman's head all the way to the floor. They were those big, fat flakes that occur when snow first starts to fall on a cold winter's day. But in a house?

"Perhaps it's some strange kind of dust in the air," suggested Mrs. Koch.

"No," said the guest firmly, "because I am all wet." And she *was* all wet.

The men checked the windows to see if anything from outside might be blowing in, but no windows were open; anyway, it was not raining or snowing or blowing or anything outside. Next, they climbed on chairs and examined the ceiling, in case there might be some sort of leak up there. But there wasn't.

It was about this time that the visitors put down their Bloody Marys and took their departure. Who, after all, wants to sit around and be snowed on? But then, and here's the best evidence that this was a supernormal manifestation, as the lady started to go out the front door, the same thing happened again. It snowed, not quite so heavily, but just as definitely. So after all, it was not something leaking from the living room ceiling.

On occasion, any of us would like to have a household ghost, or gremlin at least, to blame for many of the things that go wrong in our houses. But, unfortunately, with us it always turns out to be the washing machine, or the plumbing, or the electric wiring, and it goes away only after a big repair bill. Not so with the Kochs. Their manifestations start—and then they just stop, and that's all there is to it. Well, not quite all. There was this one thing more. After the admiral and his wife left, the Kochs' two beagle dogs, Duncan and Douglas (not Scotties, *beagles*) came into the house. When they reached the living room they circled round and round the chair on which the lady guest had been sitting. But they never did mention what was bothering them.

The Koch dogs also figure, although passively, in the last, and possibly the best story about the old Robert E. Lee mansion. You'd think that if a strange animal got into their yard they'd bark their heads off. Of course they would. But they don't even give a yip when the little black dog with the long body and the long tail comes by—because he is obviously a ghost dog. It must first be made clear that the Koch garden is not one that just any old wandering dog can enter, or any old beagle can get out of. Beagles demand very special yards. Unless they are practically stockades with high walls that are very well grounded, a beagle can manage some way of escape, either by climbing over the fence or digging under it. But Duncan and Douglas *have* just such walls. They take great pride in their garden, too, for it is beautiful, with lots of grass and flowers and trees. If an alien animal were to break into it, Duncan and Douglas would run him out very promptly.

Yet people keep seeing the little black dog there.

"The first time I saw him," Mrs. Koch said, "I was inside the dining room, and he walked by outside the big French windows. I rushed out, thinking the gate must have been left open, but it was closed. Douglas and Duncan were both lying quietly on the paved patio outside the window, not even stirring. You know if another dog had come into their yard they'd have gone crazy. I ran out instantly, yet no dog was to be found, and my pets obviously hadn't seen a thing unusual. But I had, definitely!"

Mrs. Koch was glad when she learned that her husband had also observed the little black dog. So had a house guest. None of them knew that the others were seeing little black dogs until one day when the guest happened to ask where the *black* one was. She meant "that other one," not the beagles, the black one. She had thought it was one of the household pets. After that, Mr. Koch admitted that he had seen the animal often when he came in from the garage in the evening. Mrs. Koch felt much better.

All the descriptions agree as to the appearance of the ghost dog— a mixture that looks like longhaired dachshund and some sort of terrier. He has a long body and short legs, and short floppy ears. He has a long, hairy tail, too, which is always wagging. The fact that he gets along so well with the beagles makes it seem inevitable that he is such a fixture around there that they pay no more attention to him than to each other. One suspects he's there to play with the little ghost children, whose lively laughter lilts so merrily in the old Lee home.

CHAPTER THREE

THE WHALEY HOUSE

WHO WAS "YANKEE JIM" ROBINSON and why would he want to haunt a house in which he had never set foot? Is the mere fact that he was hanged on the property sufficient to cause him to continue to hang around in the house subsequently constructed on the premises? This is one of the mysteries to be unraveled at the Whaley House in "Old Town," San Diego, California.

Although not large by eastern American or European standards at the time it was completed in 1857, Thomas Whaley's house was considered to be the "most elegant" in Southern California. A San Diego pioneer, Whaley had come to California aboard the schooner "Sutton," during the Gold Rush. The trip from New York had taken 204 days. Skippered by a green navigator, the ship had hazardous adventures rounding Cape Horn, and was subjected to a variety of additional troubles, including losing its figurehead and two passengers—one fell overboard and another committed suicide. After two years in San Francisco, Thomas Whaley went to San Diego and established a business. Two years later he returned to New York, married Anna Eloise deLaunay, and brought his bride back to San Diego.

It took Whaley a year to finish building his house, because, like an old plantation house of the Deep South, it was constructed of materials to be found on its own grounds. Bricks used in the building came from a clay-bed and kiln—the first brickyard in San Diego—which Thomas Whaley established on his own property.

The builder could hardly have suspected when he designed the large room on the north end of the house as a granary without flooring that, eventually, it would be employed variously as a school-room, a Protestant church, and a theater for a traveling company,

"The Tanner Troupe." It was also the San Diego County Court-house for a time. Much of old San Diego's social life also centered around this home. When President Ulysses S. Grant and Benjamin Harrison visited in San Diego, they stayed with the Whaleys. And Union General Thomas Sedgwick was quartered there at one time.

The Whaley House would be gone today except for a group of San Diegoans who prevented its demolition in 1956 by forming a Historical Shrine Foundation of San Diego County and buying the land and the building. Later, the same group convinced the County of San Diego that the house should be preserved as a historical museum and restored to its early condition.

During the time that the restoration was in progress, June Reading, director of the Whaley House, and her husband, Jim, made an early morning inspection of the work. As they stood together in the downstairs hall in bright daylight, both heard the sound of footsteps on the floor above. It was too early for workmen to be about, so the Readings quickly made a thorough search. They saw no one, and they also determined that all the doors and windows were securely locked from the inside. Yet, as they toured the house, the sound of heavy boots tramping down the stairs could be heard.

According to local tradition, the one who checks most thoroughly through the house to make sure those doors and windows are care-fully locked every night is a ghost. But she would hardly be tramp-ing around in heavy boots, for she is a small woman answering the description of Anna Whaley. She is said to glide silently about the house carrying a candle. Perhaps the heavy-footed phantom is her husband—or he may be Yankee Jim Robinson.

Mrs. Reading was so impressed by her unusual experiences in the house that she went to Kay Sterner, president of the California Parapsychological Association, for information. Mrs. Sterner, a psy-chic, visited the house and herself saw the little lady with the candle, wearing the old-fashioned dress of the mid-nineteenth cen-tury. The ghost actually brushed past Mrs. Sterner, seeming not to notice her, as she made her tour of investigation of the window fastenings and door locks.

Kay Sterner was also startled to see the apparition of a man hanging in the archway between the reading room and the parlor. He, too, was dressed in the clothing of an earlier generation—the generation of Yankee Jim.

In 1852, the time of Jim's death, San Diego was not known as a "hanging town"; but his crime was evidently so grave that he hung for it. What Jim had done was to attempt to steal the only pilot boat in the harbor—the "Plutus"—and that must have been considered a heinous outrage to those who would have been left bereft of pilot boats if he had succeeded. It was an awfully inept crime, though, all the way around. It would make a hilarious episode in a Western movie. In the first place, when Yankee Jim started out to steal the boat he was wearing a bright red shirt, which would seem to have been a bad tactic right off. In the second place, he was observed by the owner of the pilot boat, a Mr. Keating, as he was rowing toward the "Plutus." Keating, standing on the wharf and seeing a suspicious-looking man in a red shirt much too close to his boat, realized that something dishonest must be afoot. He considered the matter carefully for a full second, and then fired a shot over Yankee Jim's rowboat, calling out to him to come in so that he could be apprehended. Instead, Jim rowed to shore somewhere else and escaped. Keating rushed for the law, and a posse started out in pursuit. What follows is reported in the San Diego *Herald* of August 27, 1852.

Mr. Reiner, our indefatigable deputy Sheriff, proceeded on as far as Rose's Ranch, and hearing nothing of him, he gave orders to the Mexican having charge of the place that if he should happen to see any wayfaring man with a red shirt on pass that way, he must use every exertion to arrest him. The Sheriff's knowledge of Spanish being somewhat limited, and having a broad Hungarian accent, the Mexican understood him to say that if any suspicious looking hombre, with a red shirt on, came along the road he must take him dead or alive! and bring him to town.

About twelve o'clock that night, the Mexican made his appearance on the Plaza, with a man tied on a mule and his head tied up in a handkerchief. Upon being examined, he proved to be the identical individual that Keating fired at from the wharf (the red shirt was still on him). The Mexican stated that the man came to his house just after dark and asked for something to eat—that he afterwards laid down, but seeing some movements on the part of the Mexican which excited his suspicion, he made for the door and attempted to escape, whereupon the Mexican's wife handed him a riata and an old artillery sword, and they both joined in the chase. For the first hundred yards it was about an even race between "red shirt" and the Mexican. The latter then began to gain, and pretty soon the riata might have been seen describing circles over the Mexican's head, then away it went whizzing through the air with fatal precision, and down came the noose over the body of "Yankee Jim," pinning his arms close to his sides. Jim did not seem to relish this being brought up with a "round turn," and commenced struggling to free himself from his toils, but was soon brought to the ground by a tremendous blow on the head with the old rusty sword, making a most ghastly wound just above the ear which would have killed him but for the protection of a thick hat. He was then bound with strong cords, lashed upon a mule and brought to town.

Less than a month later Jim was hanged, and even that was a more uncomfortable proceeding than necessary. The scaffold, erected on the property on which the Whaley House was later built, was defective and Jim dropped only five feet, being strangled instead of having his neck broken properly. Jim was left hanging for forty-five minutes, as an example to the townspeople, who never since have attempted to steal a pilot boat. It would seem to have been rather rough treatment for such a crime; and, according to Frances Bardacke, author of "The Swinging World of 'Yankee Jim'" (*San Diego Magazine,* January 1966), perhaps the reason so little was recorded about it is that the town felt embarrassed at having meted out such severe punishment for a relatively minor infraction of the law. Two other men were later captured and implicated as Jim's partners in the robbery attempt, but they were let off lightly.

Was there something in Jim's past that made the law in San Diego so eager to rid the world of this disreputable character? It is difficult to know. Occasionally there are persons in history who appear mysteriously, lend their names to certain places or events, and then disappear. When Yankee Jim disappeared at the end of a rope his legend remained, but all facts that existed about his life vanished with him. He has since been reputed to have been either a gentleman or a desperado from "up north." Was he actually James Loring Robinson, an eastern man of culture who had fallen on evil times, or was he a burly, six-foot-three-inch-tall Nova Scotian named

Santiago Robinson? Or might he have been the individual in the Sacramento version of the "Yankee Jim" story, a man who founded a once-prosperous town in the mother lode country named "Yankee Jim's Diggings"? In that case he would not have been a French Canadian at all but a "Sydney Duck," and, as Fran Bardacke says, "You didn't call a man a Sydney Duck unless you wore a gun and knew how to use it . . . fast." These men were deported criminals from the penal colonies of Australia, and they were rough and tough. But if either Canadian or Australian, why did Jim have the sobriquet "Yankee" attached to his name? Why did he end up swinging for committing a small crime in San Diego? And, though justifiably annoyed, why is he now still swinging?

Lillian Whaley, the youngest of Thomas and Anna's six children, who died in 1953 at the age of eighty-nine, was the last person to live in the Whaley House; and she lived downstairs only. In her memoirs is a letter in which she states that so many strange things took place in her old home that she was afraid to sleep upstairs. She felt a force in the upper rooms that didn't want her. It disturbed her sleep and made her uncomfortable.

Friends of Lilly Whaley have confirmed her fears to this extent— when they called on her in the house and were sitting chatting with her in the parlor, sounds of footsteps could plainly be heard in the rooms above. These sounds were heard again as recently as June 1966, when the Theatre Arts Guild of San Diego City College staged an original play entitled "Yankee Jim" in the courtroom of the Whaley House. The play centered on the trial of Yankee Jim and its characters were the townspeople involved, among whom was Thomas Whaley. After the play was over and the public and all the cast had gone home, the sound of footsteps in the old house was so unnerving that the young lady who stayed to count the night's receipts refused to remain there alone.

Lilly Whaley always maintained that it was Yankee Jim who haunted the house. But June Reading says, "I am sure that Thomas and Anna Whaley are also here." She believes that the ninth step of the stairway is somehow associated with the ghost, or ghosts. It is where a woman has been seen, and in that spot June herself has walked into what seemed to be a cobweb or a bit of Saran Wrap; but nothing was visible there.

Grace Gourguin, a volunteer guide at the museum, independently confirms June's stories, although she says she has never had any personal psychic experiences and does not believe in ghosts. "But I know what I heard," she says. "Mrs. Reading and I sat eating our lunch at a table in the downstairs hall and we heard the sound of heavy boots upstairs. We ran up and looked, but there was nothing, and no one there." And they have carefully observed every creak and groan of the old house to compare it with the walking sounds. "Another time," Mrs. Gourguin goes on, "I had just taken a large group through the house and was standing downstairs with my hand on the newel post of the stairway. I thought I saw someone standing upstairs, just for an instant. But there was no one upstairs in the house."

Mrs. Reading's most curious experience occurred when a class of children from the Chula Vista School were being taken through the house. She was talking to them in the old courtroom, with the children grouped in front of her and their teachers and the bus driver behind them. She says, "The children were paying such unusually good attention to me, and were so much quieter than youngsters usually are, that I was quite inspired. I went into a long and involved story about Whaley's adventures on the ship coming out here."

When she had finished her talk, June learned the reason for the rapt attention. She was told by pupils, teachers, and bus driver alike, "While you were talking the chain began to move up and down." The chain, which was near her side, but which she was in no way touching, is used to keep people from walking into the end of the room where the judge's bench sits. The spectator seats in the courtroom are separated from the counsel table and judge's bench by an elaborate balustrade that extends across the entire room except for a passageway about three feet wide. The chain is fastened across this opening between the railing and the wall. It is composed of links so heavy it could in no way swing of its own accord unless set into motion by some extremely strong vibration. Yet as June was speaking the chain had lifted up and down, as if simulating the movement of waves. Then it had swung back and forth. This action continued during most of her talk.

Mrs. Reading and others have confirmed that there is no vibration from cars or trucks going by outside the house which is strong enough to cause movement of objects inside. But unaccountable things still go on. One of June's oft-told tales is that on Sunday mornings, right after time for church services to be over, she often hears the sound of the front door opening and people coming into the house—when no one is there to be seen. She thinks it is the Whaley family returning from church, still repeating activities that were meaningful to them when they were alive. She says that if she is psychic she does not know it, but "Particularly since I have been in the Whaley House I have had these feelings, and I believe them."

One of the most interesting experiences to be reported in this place involves a group of about fifteen college students. They are all members of a semi-professional musical comedy group who call themselves "The Starlight Opera," and they became interested in the house because of the ghost stories told them by one of their members, nineteen-year-old Bill Richardson, who used to be a guide there. On Friday, August 13, 1965, a night of a full moon, they held a seance in the house, accompanied by Jim and June Reading. Meeting first in the parlor, they sat around for a while singing songs of Civil War days, to make the ghosts in the house feel at home. Then a brief talk was given by Caroline White of the California Parapsychology Foundation, who explained that they were not to be afraid, no matter what occurred. "All the manifestations in a haunted house follow natural laws and are not 'supernormal,'" she said. "It is just that the natural laws they obey are not yet understood by science and can't be explained in terms of what we at present know of the world."

After this, the group sat silently for a few moments. There were no windows or doors open in the house, but they felt cool breezes. Then a light appeared, floating above the head of one of the girls. After that a shadow became visible on the wall of the reading room back of the parlor. It lasted for about fifteen minutes, changing in shape as they watched. Finally it sank to the floor and disappeared. Then the young people divided into various groups and visited other rooms of the house. At different times during the evening, Bill Richardson told me, "We heard heavy boots walking upstairs when no one was up there."

Barry Bunker said, "I went upstairs with a group into the master bedroom. Several left after a while and finally there were just four of us. Then one of the girls saw the bedspread moving. She called out, and then we all saw it. The chandelier began swinging in a pattern we were unable to duplicate when we tried it. The girl then said, 'Thank you,' and the chandelier turned at right angles."

Later in the evening Bill and Barry went into the kitchen together and watched as all the different utensils hanging on the wall in front of the fireplace started swinging in a line, one at a time. After a while all of them stopped, except for the meat cleaver. "It seemed to be moving all evening," Bill said. "Every time anyone went into the kitchen that old meat cleaver started swinging."

Mary Barnhill and Cammy Wesson were sitting in the other front bedroom. They didn't know what to expect but they were waiting for any manifestation that might occur. Oddly enough, what happened was not to anything external, but to their own bodies. "The hair on my arms rose up," Mary said. "Cammy's did too, and she said her skin started to crawl. Then mine did too. Now I know what it means when I read that these things happen to people. They happened to me."

In the early morning hours the entire group gathered in the courtroom and sat around the heavy library table. They placed their hands on it and concentrated, hoping that it would move. Nothing happened for about forty minutes and then they began to hear creaks in the table. Suddenly it tilted to one side and pushed those sitting on the other side over toward the bannisters. Then the huge table lifted completely off the floor at one corner. To make sure that no one was playing pranks, they moved the table in a similar manner by their own conscious physical effort. The table "made horrible noises and scraped on the floor," they said. Yet, when it moved of its own accord, there was very little sound of any kind except creaking. Since the students had a tape recorder running, they have these sounds as verification that what they say is true.

Also, all during this time the chain moved up and down or with a swinging motion, just as it had done for the Chula Vista pupils. The Starlighters examined the chain as carefully as they had inspected the table, the meat cleaver, and the other utensils, to make sure that nothing was rigged to make it move. Nothing was.

June Reading suggested that they sit at a smaller table to see if it would tap out messages via an alphabetical code, and it did. Although they got nothing that they felt was of any evidence, the rappings continued for some time. They spelled out the message that the writer was a girl seven years old with red hair who had never lived in the house and did not know the Whaleys. She would not tell her name but said it started with a "V." She said there were four other spirits in the house, including a baby. (A baby is said to have died in the back room, where the shadow had appeared on the wall.)

Sherry Bruce, one of the students, told me she had sat at the table with only two other people and it began to "walk around." They stood up and leaned over it, keeping their hands on it as it moved, and it walked into the kitchen, which adjoins the courtroom. As they entered the kitchen the meat cleaver started swinging again.

At about 6:00 A.M. the participants of this all-night vigil in the haunted house returned to their homes, knowing a great deal more than when they started about the strange world in which they lived. But not really sure just what it was that they knew.

CHAPTER FOUR

KENNEBUNKPORT CHARACTERS

ACT I, SCENE 1 OF THIS STORY finds the guests of producer Robert Currier seated around the dining room table of his two-hundred-year-old house, the silver gleaming, the crystal sparkling, and the ladies' faces softly shadowed by the candlelight. Mrs. Kenneth Roberts, wife of the author, says to Currier, "I love all your wonderful antiques. Your house is charming. But did you know it is full of ghosts?"

"I've often been told so," answers Bob, "but I haven't seen any of them myself."

"The little lady who keeps walking around the table, I wonder who she could be?" Mrs. Roberts continues. "And the man who is so unhappy. He's so obviously brooding over something."

The guests all begin to discuss the ghosts, although Mrs. Roberts is the only one present who can see them. During the badinage it is decided to call the unhappy invisible man "Ned" after a book some of them have recently read entitled *Dead Ned;* and the woman, who is described as looking like a Quaker, receives the name of "Nellie."

This shadowy couple always remained Ned and Nellie to the various persons who visited the Kennebunkport, Maine, house during the thirty years Currier lived there; and many people received evidences of their presence, ranging from strange noises to actual ghostly appearances.

Bob's sister, Florence, known to the world as popular singer Jane Morgan, has refused more than once to stay overnight in the house, because of the uncanny sounds she heard there. She was depressed, too, by the fact that an old coffin was kept in the dark and grisly basement—although Currier says it has rotted away in recent years.

The big barn next door houses the Kennebunkport Country Playhouse, and Robert Currier was its producer for many years, retiring from active show business just a few years ago. He now lives on nearby Blueberry Hill, where he gardens, fights gophers, raises blueberries, and crustily conducts an antique shop in Jane's big yellow house at the front of the property. His own home is furnished with many unusually magnificent early American pieces, in which he takes great pride.

The ghost house next to the Playhouse is now rented to the theater group; it is used upstairs as a dormitory for actresses and stage assistants, and downstairs for staff offices. All the young people housed there know about Ned and Nellie, but they are such a noisy, earthy crew they would frighten away any self-respecting haunt. Actually, if Nellie has seen the piles of dirty clothes, the stacks of books and letters and magazines and trash, the unmade beds, and the generally unkempt condition of the girls' rooms, her good Quaker soul has probably retreated in horror. What the modern world is coming to may be the reason for her withdrawal from society.

But if she is only a mournful memory now, Nellie was seen about the place quite often for a period of years. "Long before the war, probably about 1934," Bob Currier told me, "some actors were there. Karen Van Ryn, an actress, slept in the attic the first night. She came down the next morning saying, 'I don't think I want to sleep up there again.'" In the middle of the night she had seen a Quaker maid, wearing the typical cap and dress.

"She was awfully nice, really," insisted Karen. "She smiled at me and seemed perfectly happy. But I just don't think I want to sleep up there any more."

The attic, now bare except for a few stacks of old newspapers dating back to the 1930s, has often been the focal point of activity—whatever its source. Fred Walker of Yonkers, New York, the business manager of the Kennebunkport Playhouse, says that he once stayed a whole week alone in the house with no ghostly problems—except for the first night, when he was nearly scared to death because of noises from the attic. Since he had naturally been briefed on Ned and Nellie, he had a difficult time convincing himself the racket was not caused by ghosts, even though he says he doesn't *believe* in ghosts. The next morning, in safe daylight, he went up to investigate and found that an attic window had been left open. So obviously, he affirms, the sounds he heard were caused by birds that had blundered in.

The other area of the house that has produced odd feelings and grotesque happenings is the second-floor left front bedroom, which looks like any well-arranged, cheerful bedroom in any normal old house. But, in that room, Bob Currier says, a woman named Old Lady Wells, who was known as a witch doctor, lived. For the last twenty-four years of her life she never left the room except to take her herbs up to the attic and hang them up to dry. Old Lady Wells died in her bed at the age of one hundred and twenty-four.

Robert Currier's friend Muriel Pearce slept in this front room on her first sojourn in the house. The next morning she reported, "You know, I had a visitor last night. First I had this peculiar, but wonderful feeling, like light in the room, very white and glowing. Then a lady appeared, all done up in a Quaker costume. She was very lovely."

Bob swears that Muriel did not know of Karen Van Ryn's experience. He is sure that Nellie is an entity who can in no way be connected with Old Lady Wells, the witch doctor, and he doesn't know why it is not the old woman who is seen in her room instead of the Good Grey Ghost. It is all very confusing.

Actress Mye Eolis, who is now one of the producers of the Playhouse, has Old Lady Wells's front bedroom at present, but she is a very matter-of-fact woman who does not let herself become uncomfortable about things she cannot explain. "I can account for most of the strange noises I hear to my own satisfaction," she told me. "They can usually be credited to the creaks of old buildings, or birds in the attic, or mice in the walls." However, Mye added that there had been two strange experiences that she could not understand; she ignored them rather than calling them supernatural.

Mye said: "An associate stayed here for a while and he was using the front bedroom which is now mine. One night, about 3:00 A.M., one of the panes of glass in the front window suddenly smashed to smithereens. He examined the floor carefully, and the area all around under the window outside, but there was no rock anywhere to be found that could have done it." Mye sat thoughtfully quiet for a moment, then she added, "They have just recently had this window repaired."

Mye Eolis was personally involved in the second incident: "One time I came up to Kennebunkport from New York and was to meet a friend at the house. It had not yet been opened for the season and no one was there. Yet, as I drove up the driveway, I'm sure I saw a flickering light in the attic, as if a candle were burning up there. Naturally, I didn't want to go into the place alone, whether the light was caused by spooks or robbers, so I went in to town and met my friend. When we came back together later there was no light in the attic, and no sign that anyone had broken into the house or in any other way disturbed it. Everything was locked up snugly. Yet—and here's the part I wish you'd explain to me—we found a candle stub on the floor of the attic."

Several months after I heard these stories from Mye, I happened to run into her in a Kennebunkport restaurant. She eagerly told me the latest occurrence at the house, which involved her two cats, Smokey and Pokey.

At four-thirty on the morning of September 13, 1966, the usually quiet animals went wild. For a solid hour they stayed in the bathroom meowing and jumping up at the wall. Smokey, the male, was particularly worried about the stair well, which runs alongside the bathroom wall and up to the attic, and he leaped against it continually. Having so recently gone through this unexplainable incident with her own pets, Mye did not now sound as coolly objective about the haunts as she previously had.

Jane Morgan often talks about her experiences in this house. She has heard thumping sounds, a noise as if someone were walking when she knew no one else was there, the opening and closing of doors, and various other manifestations that she does not care to go through again. Her mother, Mrs. Olga Currier, was with her and heard the same sounds at the same times.

A Boston friend of Mrs. Currier's was a medium named Leslie Tolman, known professionally as Madame Shah. She was invited to visit the Curriers, but left in the middle of the night, absolutely afraid to stay in the house. She told Bob to get rid of the place. "They are not happy spirits here," she said. "They are evil."

Other friends, Kenneth and Mary Leathers, were uncomfortable, too. A sudden chill once hit Kenneth and he began shivering. He said to Olga Currier, "Do you feel that?" She replied, "Oh, yes, that's the ghost." Kenneth was probably just as well pleased when his wife refused to stay over in the house and they could leave before nightfall.

A few years ago some musicians brought with them the ninety-seven-year-old mother of one of them. Suddenly, during dinner, the old lady, who, it turned out, was very psychic, said, "My goodness, you have a lot of ghosts in this house."

"Do you see them?" Bob asked her.

"Yes, I just saw one that looked like a Quaker—no, she looks more like a Shaker." This made more sense to Currier, because there were many Shakers in Maine at one time, and some of the doors of his house had come from an old Shaker meeting hall.

"She is very happy," the woman went on, "but I'm distressed about the soldier who wanders in the house. He went up the chimney a while ago. He's looking for something he can't find." On one point, this lady agreed with Madame Shah. "There is great spirit influence in this house," she said.

Perhaps there is. In 1949 the theater, which was then in a barn quite close to the house, burned to the ground. Yet the house, not twenty feet away, was miraculously saved.

"I lived there alone for years," Robert Currier says, "but I didn't mind the ghosts. I used to talk to them." Since he has moved from there Currier has acquired Robespierre, a black French poodle. Whenever Robespierre is taken to the house, he barks all the time he is there. "He will never settle down in one room but constantly paces about," his master says. Dogs are usually very sensitive to ghosts.

"I had a cook," Bob says, "well, not exactly a cook—she was a woman who taught piano and coached singers—but she liked to cook for me here in the summers. Her name was Janet Hessler, and she believed in using the ouija board to try to communicate with spirits. She tried it here and it wrote that Nellie was unhappy because she wanted to marry Bob Currier." Of course, most ouija board communications are not to be trusted and Bob knew it; but just in case it would make his Quaker-Shaker friend happy, Bob spoke to a preacher about whether or not it would be possible for him to be married to a ghost. The preacher said he wouldn't mind performing the ceremony, but he was not sure just how his church would react. Anyway, Bob never got around to doing anything about it.

A young man named Darryl diShurley came to work with the group about six years ago. He now has his own home on Blueberry Hill, but for a while he lived in the haunted house. His story about his experiences there starts as he arrived at the house for the first time; and he swears that he had never heard a word about its peculiarities.

"As we drove up to the house around the circular drive," he says, "I glanced up toward the attic windows. I had been told that the house was vacant, but I saw somebody there. 'Who's the lady upstairs looking out the third-story window?' I asked.

"'Nobody,' answered Bob, 'there's no one in the house.'

"I certainly saw her," Darryl insists. "She had on a white cap and a big white collar. She looked like a Quaker or a Puritan."

On another occasion, Darryl says, "I was sitting in the music room listening to the stereo. I suddenly felt the presence of someone coming through the archway to my right. I could see the outline of her but she was transparent, like a negative. She sat down in the chair by the side of the door, and I watched her. A few moments later she had disappeared."

DiShurley was asked if he usually saw ghosts, but he replied that his experiences in this house were the first he had ever had of this type. "There were times when I was frightened of her," he says. "I have walked in the side door and started to run up the stairway opposite it and have seen the bottom of her dress above me. For some reason this has usually made me uneasy. Yet, I spent a summer in that front bedroom and had but one strange experience. It was in the middle of the night when I suddenly sat straight up in bed wide awake. I couldn't see anything, but I felt someone come in one door, circle the bed, and go out the other door. There was no noise involved with this incident, just the strong feeling of a presence."

It is obvious that whatever is going on there does not seem designed to pacify anyone. Janet Hessler's ouija board may have been right when it once wrote that the ghosts there don't like actors or theater people. Perhaps they will not settle down until the theater people give it up and go away. But, because of the success of the Kennebunkport Country Playhouse, that may be a long time in the future.

CHAPTER FIVE

THE MYSTERY HOUSE
OF SANTA CLARA VALLEY

IN CALIFORNIA, less than 150 miles apart, are two houses that epito-mize the extremes of taste in the use of money. One is William Randolph Hearst's beautiful San Simeon, an elaborate testimony to the sane expenditure of millions of dollars in the construction of a monumental palace. The second, in San Jose, is a building known as the Winchester Mystery House, or the Mystery House of Santa Clara Valley, a pathetic $5,000,000 witness to an obviously de-ranged mind.

The 160-room mansion of mystery was allegedly designed at the instigation of spirits of the dead, and it has never been in-habited by anybody else but them, except for one lonely woman and her servants. Now, it is a dejected showplace where tourists who want to gape at the oddities of its construction pay $1.50 apiece for the slightly depressing pleasure.

The story of this curious residence begins around the middle of the nineteenth century in New Haven, Connecticut, where charm-ing, gregarious Sarah L. Winchester lived happily with her husband and only daughter. Sarah was the devoted wife of William Wirt Win-chester, son and heir of the "rifle king," the Honorable Fisher Winchester. Sarah was a very tiny person, well under five feet tall, delicate and slender, alert and vivacious.

When tragedy struck this woman, it pulled no punches. Her hus-band died a lingering death from tuberculosis, and her little girl passed away almost immediately afterward. Shocked and numbed by grief, her only interest in life gone, Sarah was desolate. Friends tried to console her, but she saw no reason to live and had no hope for the future.

Finally, because of her lifelong interest in the occult, she was lured out of her home to attend a service of the Boston medium Adam Coons. And there a miracle happened to her.

"Your husband is here," the medium said, and gave a description of William Wirt Winchester that was startling in its exactness. "He is standing right beside you, can't you see him?"

"Oh, if only I could," Sarah moaned. She had gone to this medium anonymously. How could he know she had just lost her husband and what he looked like? Sarah was more intrigued than she would let herself admit.

"Tell him I miss him desperately," she told Coons, who relayed her message. Then he said, "He wants you to know he is with you and that he will always be with you." He then proceeded to give her the message that changed her entire life. He said, "This is a warning. You will be haunted forever by the ghosts of those who have been killed by Winchester rifles, unless you make amends to them." She was told that she must sell all her property in the east and head toward the setting sun, firmly guided all the way by her husband.

"When you see the right house you will know. Buy it, no matter how much it costs, and make room in it for all these spirits." She was told that she would have to add rooms to the house constantly to provide shelter for the ever increasing number of victims of the Winchester guns. But that would not be a disadvantage, her husband said, because as long as she continued to build she would continue to live.

If anyone doubts the story of Sarah's conversation with the medium, or feels that the various newspaper and magazine accounts of her interest in spirit communication and ghosts are unfounded, he has only to follow her history from then on. The mess she made of the home she built is evidence enough. Could there be any other explanation for her mad actions? And why else did she construct a seance room with no windows in the center of the building? I feel quite assured in going along with the data put out for tourists of her home, that she felt she had to make amends to the spirits of those whom her guns had killed. Perhaps it is not too far-fetched a sentiment for any rifle manufacturer to confess to; although those who supply the world with firearms, bombs, and other lethal weapons may not at the moment agree with me.

Judging from all her subsequent actions, Sarah L. Winchester was completely convinced that she had been talking with the actual spirit of her husband, and she was never to doubt it again. In complete faith that her anguished prayers for help had been answered by him, she decided to devote every remaining hour of her life to a labor of love and sacrifice. She would give up everything she had, if it were necessary, to make recompense to those poor individuals whose lives had been snuffed out permaturely by the weapons invented and produced by her husband's family.

Sarah sold her home in New Haven and, with a $20,000,000 fortune at her disposal, set out toward the West, with an abiding faith that she would be guided by her husband for the rest of her life. After a long and searching journey, she finally entered California, where she began to sense that her trail was ending. When she finally saw a seventeen-room home under construction on a thirty-acre estate in the magnificent Santa Clara Valley, she realized, with a joyful lift of spirit, that this was the place to which she had been directed. She immediately negotiated with its owner, a Dr. Caldwell, for the purchase of the property, and began to plan alterations and additions to the house. She retained the physician's architect and head carpenter, but only for a time. When they began to realize the eccentricity of her desires, they both quit in indignation.

Sarah's fortune might have remained more solvent had more building tradesmen been as reluctant to serve her. But for the munificent salaries she offered she had no difficulty finding men who would work under any conditions. Actually, she had no real need to worry about money. Her income was quite adequate to meet the $1,000 a day she spent on the house. In fact, her royalties from rifle sales came to more than $1,000 a day. And in those times there were no income taxes or inheritance taxes.

So Mrs. Winchester had her pick of help as she added to her wonder house constantly for thirty-six years, building and rebuilding, altering and changing, tearing down and putting up. Twenty-two carpenters worked the year round. One parquetry expert did nothing for thirty-three years but lay floors and pick them up again, or in other ways juggle choice mosaics of wood throughout the house. Another craftsman built cupolas for thirty years. The sound of hammer and saw never stopped during daylight hours, even on Sundays and holidays, as the original seventeen rooms were supplemented until there were one hundred sixty in all. And of all these rooms, not one dozen are on the same level.

Here, in the largest private home in the world, Sarah lived in splendor. Her staff of eighteen servants kept the place immaculate for her unseen guests, but for no others, since visitors were never allowed inside the doors. Outside, in the parklike grounds, twelve Japanese gardeners planted and cared for the imported trees, flowers, and shrubbery. They constantly strove to make hedges higher and thicker, to keep out the peeking public. How well they succeeded is indicated by the fact that today nothing but the tip-top towers are visible from outside the grounds. And the growth is so thick close to the house that its contours are difficult to determine.

As rooms were added to rooms, wings grew onto wings, doors joined windows, ells augmented annexes, and peaks were appended to spires, the mansion took on the look of a crazy house in an amusement park. It still looks that way today. Inside things are even sillier. There are three elevators, forty-seven fireplaces, countless stairways going nowhere, a blind chimney that stops just short of the ceiling, closets and cupboards that open onto blank walls or into space, balconies of every description, trap doors, and secret double-back passageways. There are skylights one above another, elevators that creep only short distances, and doors which open to sudden drops to a glass roof or to the yard below. There is one stairway, built inside a closet, that ends against the blank wall. Additional oddities of the house include the fact that all the posts inside are installed upside down, and that many of the bathrooms have either glass or screen doors.

The number 13 is predominant everywhere, because Sarah was convinced that it had an uncanny potency to hold in check the bad spirits she also had to contend with. Chandeliers have 13 lights, ceilings have 13 panels, rooms have 13 windows. There are 13 baths; and most of the forty stairways have 13 steps. Many of these steps are only two and one-half inches deep. One stairway, constructed like a maze, has seven flights and requires forty-four steps to go ten feet.

The reason for these curious building techniques made sense to Sarah: it was to control the evil entities and keep them from harming her. After all, some of the victims of her guns had been "badmen" of the West, or malicious criminals of the city slums. They certainly had not reformed just because they had passed into spirit life. And so she had to watch out for them at all times. She received her instructions at seances every night as to what new tricks to build into the house in order to frustrate them.

But Sarah also had to make happy the good spirits who inhabited her domicile, so her efforts were not all farcical. In addition to the bizarre there is also the beautiful and expensive in this eccentric palace. There are gold and silver chandeliers; exquisite parquetry floors; art glass windows and doors inlaid with German silver; Belgian crystal; Swiss art-molded bronze bathtubs; Carrara marble; and many spectacular Tiffany glass windows valued at $1,000 each. For some unknown reason, they are all concave and convex. Two of these stained-glass windows in what is called the ballroom (although the only parties ever held there were for the benefit of ghosts) are engraved with quotations from Shakespeare: "Wide unclasp the tables of their thoughts," says one; and "These same thoughts people this little world," says the other. What the significance of these messages was for Sarah, or for her spirit friends, has never been revealed.

After her death, warehouses on the property were found to contain a wealth of supplies awaiting Sarah L. Winchester's planned continuation of her life-sustaining building program. Among the stored treasures were light fixtures; sash and doors; hardware; art glass windows and doors; cedar, oak, ash, walnut, maple, cherry, mahogany, and rosewood interior finish of the finest; screens; tile; plumbing—everything bought, catalogued, and stored by a woman who believed that their addition to her home would bring her immortality.

Sarah slept in a different bedroom every night until she ran out of changes, and then she began all over again. But one special, multi-windowed salon was her favorite. On its walls was embossed French wallpaper. It was draped with the richest of white satin, emblematic of Sarah's spiritual purity. Even the floor was especially designed, its inlaid parquetry changing color tones as the window light reflected on it from different angles.

Sarah's need for heat was ever present because of her intense arthritic pains. That is why she had one room planned to produce as much heat as possible. It has numerous radiator vents and several fireplaces, as well as many windows to let in the sunlight. This spa was built in her own home because she would not go outside to travel to a health resort. During all the years she lived there, she was observed in town only once. At that time, someone took her picture in her buggy. Sitting there swathed in robes, she looked like a regal little Queen Victoria. Sarah never once entered another building or church, never rode on a bus or train. The only time she was forced to leave her home for a while, after the San Francisco earthquake, she was transported away in her own carriage.

Mrs. Winchester never once paid a friendly visit to anyone. Nor did she want people to enter her home. Any well-meaning stranger who might have attempted to be neighborly was discouraged at the front door by the resplendent but austere butler, who announced a coldly formal, "Madame is indisposed." The time eventually arrived when the front door was ordered locked and boarded up, and it has never been used again.

Several famous persons are reported to have called upon Sarah, however. Among these was President Theodore Roosevelt, a firearms enthusiast. Roosevelt dropped by for a friendly chat while on a western tour, but whether or not he got it is questionable. His whole entourage was conducted to the back door and left there. Perhaps it was to the famous carriage house that they were shown. It has doorways wide enough for an entire presidential party, for they were designed so that Sarah's horse and carriage could enter the house. From this room several passageways of normal size lead into other areas; but there is also one door just five feet tall—the private entrance for the tiny mistress.

Another prominent visitor was religious leader Mary Baker Eddy, who was given short shrift. But we are told that magician Harry Houdini was made to feel at home. Perhaps this was because of his authentic, if negative, interest in Spiritualism. One can only wish it were possible to learn what his reaction was if he was shown through this fantastic abode. Could it be possible that he was even allowed to enter the famous Blue Room, that small and secret seance chamber where none but the lady of the house had ever set foot since its completion? There she sat nightly, wearing long robes embossed with esoteric designs, holding seances for no one but herself and her spirit guides and companions.

Every night a melancholy summons bell in a tower with wide-hanging eaves rang out on the stroke of midnight, inviting the shades of the dead to come to the meeting. It is said they had frequent parties, too. Banquets were held regularly in the large bird's-eye-maple-paneled dining hall with the gold-and-silverleaf-decorated walls. Here Sarah happily presided, the thirteenth, naturally, along with her twelve honored phantom guests. She personally served them on solid gold plates, part of a $30,000 service, offering them pheasant under glass, caviar, truffles, and other gourmet viands that had been carefully prepared in the six kitchens by chefs she had brought from Paris and Vienna.

Hints of her employees' rotundity make it appear distinctly possible that any food untasted by the select company of shadowy wraiths was later consumed by the servants. If this was true, they deserved it. Sarah paid exceedingly well in order to get anyone to remain there with her, and so, once hired, a servant seldom left her. But they all must have more than earned every cent they made, running at her beck and call up and down the many whimsical stairways and dark passages of that creepy rabbit-warren.

One night in 1906, Sarah was awakened by the tipping of her bed, the buckling of the floor, the rattling and shattering of doors and windows, and the crashing of wood as the structures on the roof flattened and fell.

"Oh, God help me," she cried in panic. "The evil spirits have taken over the house." Even after all she had done to discourage them, and to pacify them, they had finally turned on her and were tearing her home apart. Terrified, she rushed to the internal communication system by which she usually was able to summon help. It recorded her call, but not where she was. After her servants had extricated themselves from whatever disorder the earthquake had caused them, they began to search for their mistress; but they did not know which of the many bedrooms she was sleeping in that night. While they hunted for her, avoiding crashing walls and stepping around debris, Sarah cowered in her bed, frightened almost to annihilation. The poor little soul probably would not have been nearly so alarmed if she had known that a natural calamity was occurring. To her it was a personal vengeance being inflicted upon her for those hated Winchester rifles.

After several hours of horrifying imprisonment, Sarah finally was rescued, a whimpering wreck. She was never to set foot in that bedroom again.

"Board it up!" she ordered imperiously, as soon as she had regained her composure. "No, don't go in there for a thing. Leave it the way it is." And so, for the next sixteen years, the room remained closed, with her bedding, clothing, and toiletries untouched.

Actually, the house realized considerably less damage than most of the property in that area. It had been so well constructed that only a few rooms were badly harmed, although some dozen or so towers and cupolas toppled. It was the mind of its owner that was shattered beyond repair. The tattered remnants of her reason completely gone, Sarah functioned with even less coherence from then on.

If the evil spirits could do that to her, she decided, then their warnings that a great flood would soon engulf the entire world must also be taken seriously. She prepared herself for this new catastrophe, quickly having a large houseboat built on a tract of land she owned some distance to the north. There she moved as soon as it was completed, and there she lived in exile for six years, restlessly waiting for the rising tide that would snuff out the lives of everyone not fortified for watery existence.

Finally deciding that she might as well meet her fate in the home she loved, Sarah returned to her nightmare mansion to carry on her life's occupation of planning, projecting, and building. And there she remained, following her usual routine, until, one day in September 1922, death caught up with her after all. She was eighty-five years old, and had lived over half her life in her lonely sepulchre.

Sarah L. Winchester left all her possessions to her niece, Margaret Merriam of Palo Alto, to whom she had turned over the business management of the estate many years before. Miss Merriam was instructed to see that the ghosts of yesteryear would continue to be properly welcome in the house. True to the trust placed in her, she even had Sarah's coffin carried out through the back door, because of Sarah's consistent refusal to use the front entrance. Eventually Miss Merriam sold the house, but with the stipulation that the new owner would keep the property in good repair and tell all comers about Sarah's devoted project.

As good as his word, the present proprietor has recently installed over five hundred miles of sprinkler-system pipe at a cost of $50,000. In order to recoup this sum, he allows visitors to tread their way through the labyrinthine corridors and up and down the well-worn stairways of the house on hourly tours. They are conducted by polite college students, and each tour covers a mile and a half's distance—all right inside the building. Visitors are warned to stay with their party because anyone who gets lost in the careworn old house may have difficulty finding his way out again.

To be alone in this place would not be so bad during the day, although a certain chill seems to be in the atmosphere even at the sunniest noontime. But no one would want to be left there after dark. Then the mystery house of the Santa Clara Valley reverts once again to its original intent—the private haunt of the ghosts of people who were killed by Winchester rifles. And Sarah then is as busy as she ever was, entertaining thirteen for dinner at the stroke of midnight.

CHAPTER SIX

ELIZABETH OF
THE FORTY ACRES

WHICH ELIZABETH HAUNTS THE BISHOP HUNTINGTON HOUSE? There were three who lived there in early days, and any one of them might be the culprit. So, for that matter, might Phyllis, the slave who died there, or any of the elderly relatives who passed on in life's ordinary procedure. But, for some unknown reason, it is an Elizabeth who always gets the blame. Some people may think a phantom who tucks the children into bed at night is going a bit too far; but the rest of her shenanigans were rather innocuous, so those who lived in the house since the manifestations started just put up with their Elizabeth and did not worry too much about her.

Now that it is a historic museum, this residence, which is known by its various titles as "Forty Acres," "The Porter, Phelps, Huntington Mansion," or "The Bishop Huntington House," on Route 47 at Hadley, Massachusetts, is open to the public in the afternoons for a fee. This gives a visitor the opportunity to enjoy not only a tour through an authentic Colonial house, but also, perhaps, a new-dimensional experience of his own. No frightening adventure occurred on my trip; but there was just enough in a nebulous sort of way to convince me that sometimes more may be encountered in a ghost house than regularly meets the eye.

The story of this beautiful estate begins with a group of English pioneers who left their homes in 1629 for the new country across the sea. After settling briefly in Dorchester on Massachusetts Bay, they continued to move on during a period of thirty years until they found the perfect spot to locate permanently. In 1659 they discovered a mile-long stretch of flat, rich meadow where the Connecticut River formed a wide arc. They delightedly colonized there, and named it Hadley. It was necessary to build a stockade immediately, because the Great River (as it was then called) was used as a high-way by the Indians who were still coming down from Canada and making raids. The area outside the town was divided up into definite tracts of common land, jointly owned by all the settlers. They would go outside to farm during the day, but were always back safely inside the stockade by nightfall.

The first marriage in Hadley joined Aaron Cooke and Sarah Westwood. Their daughter Hannah married Samuel Porter, Jr., the first male child to have been born in the town. He was from the second wealthiest family in that entire part of the Massachusetts Bay Colony, due in part to the fact that his father owned one of the two stills in Hampshire County. Even in those days, "Demon Rum" was already big business. The Porters gradually acquired title to all the common land north of the village, which was known then as "the Forty Acres and its Skirts." Although this couple wanted to build a home of their own on this property, they did not yet dare to live outside the stockade, because of the continuing danger from Indians.

The situation was safer by the time that Moses Porter, their grandson, was ready to make a home for his wife Elizabeth. He chose a lovely spot in the midst of the Forty Acres to build the first substantial house north of the town. About its beginnings, Dr. James Lincoln Huntington, one of their descendants, says in his book, *Forty Acres,* "On May 27, 1752, with due ceremony and probably a barrel of rum, the roof was raised. The main house consisted of two stories with the usual peaked roof . . . The outside boards were unpainted and grooved to suggest blocks of stone—a device called rustication. One of the original outside doors, the south door to the ell, is in its original position today."

Among many other priceless early relics there are two quaint cooking fireplaces, a smoke oven upstairs, and next to it a room with wide whitewashed board walls and a simple bed with a trundle bed underneath it. Many alterations have been made through the years, but much of the original house remains. In the dooryard south of the house Moses Porter planted three American elm trees, one for each member of the family—himself, his four-year-old daughter Betty, and his wife Elizabeth. Among the lush land-scaping that has been done since, and despite 214 years, hurricanes, and floods, one of these elms still stands. Perhaps this hardy survivor is an associate of another who is equally as indomitable, although invisible—the first Elizabeth. Certainly she had an experience heart-breaking enough to make a ghost out of anyone.

Three years after they had moved into the new house, Moses Porter left his wife and Betty, who was then seven years old, and went off to fight the French and their Indian allies. A jaunty young captain dressed in a rich and showy uniform, he was blissfully unaware that he was heading into the last battle of his short life. But early on the morning of September 8, 1755, the scouting party of which he was a member was ambushed by Indians near the southern end of Lake George in New York. Most of the men were killed, including all of the officers, in what has gone down in history as the Battle of the Bloody Morning Scout.

All the houses outside of stockades in those days had unusual window shutters which were built inside the casements. The shutters were slid across the windows at night, or in times of siege, to cover the entire area tightly, and were considered to be the best protection against marauding Indians. But there were peaceful Indians at that time, too, and one was Captain Porter's bodyservant. One night, as Elizabeth was putting Betty to bed in the northeast downstairs bedroom, she heard a knock on the heavy shutter. She pushed it back, and her husband's Indian servant ceremoniously and sadly handed Moses' sword in through the window to her. Without a word, Elizabeth accepted the weapon, understanding the significance of the act. This sword, in its original scabbard but minus its hilt, is to be seen today lying on the mantelpiece in that room in which mother and daughter received the tragic news.

It is said that the shock of this experience stayed with little Betty all her life, and caused her always to grieve for her father. Would she still continue to grieve in the house over two hundred years later? Perhaps the mother, who remained a widow all the rest of her life, would have a more genuine claim to that idiosyncrasy.

Anyway, *somebody* still sleeps in the four-poster bed in that downstairs front bedroom—the same "field bed" into which Betty was being tucked the night her father's sword came home. The covers on that bed occasionally show the impress of some frail body. Even when they are smoothed, the indentations return. Dr. James Huntington describes such an incident: "A few years ago, the canopied bed in the downstairs bedroom . . . showed the imprint of a stretched-out figure. The pillow was deeply indented as if a head had been there and the counterpane was wrinkled. The marks returned again and again every time the bed and the pillow were smoothed. This lasted for several days and the visitor who had been given this bedroom asked to sleep in another part of the house."

When Betty was sixteen she began to keep a weekly journal in which she recorded the texts of the two sermons she heard each Sunday. Later she enlarged her notes to include the events in the life of her family, thus preserving a rather complete picture of her times. Betty's account was sometimes sketchy in surprising places. She mentions only casually that a certain Charles Phelps, a young man of good family, came there occasionally on business. It is mildly startling to a reader of her journal, therefore, when she suddenly becomes engrossed in preparations for her wedding in 1770 to this same Charles Phelps. Some girls won't tell even their *diaries* all their secrets.

The third Elizabeth in this series was born to Betty and Charles in 1779, and she was fortunately given a middle name which helps to identify her in the records—she was always referred to as Elizabeth Whiting Phelps. Her picture hangs on the wall in the living room—known as the "Long Room." It is of a young woman who is wearing a white dress with a soft white fichu around her neck, frilled on the edges. Her hair is piled high, and little curls escape onto her forehead. So attired, she should look coy and cute, but her expression is unnecessarily forbidding as she looks at you out of the corner of her eyes and purses her mouth. To be frank, if less than kind, I must admit that she looks like someone who could haunt a house.

Elizabeth Whiting married Dan Huntington, another descendant of those same early settlers. This couple had eleven children. The youngest, Frederic, was elected Bishop of Central New York and moved with his family to the city of Syracuse. But he returned to Hadley every summer for long vacations, and the house at Forty Acres has taken on his name.

Early in James Lincoln Huntington's childhood he began to absorb from both grandparents the lore of their remarkable old house and the stories about his ancestors. Here he relates a delicious incident that shows something very surprising about the table manners of prominent American bishops of those days: "Sometimes, when my aunts chanced to be away, my grandfather would pour his tea into his saucer and drink from it; his wife would say, 'Bishop, what are you doing?' He would reply with a twinkle of those keen gray eyes, 'Hannah, I am drinking from my saucer.' More than once I have seen him carry food from his plate to his mouth on a knife, at which his wife would exclaim, 'Frederic, what are you doing?' He would calmly reply, 'Hannah, I am eating with my knife.'" Dr. Huntington adds that in spite of this willful behavior, the Bishop was a courtly old fellow with polished manners.

Dr. James Huntington is the member of the family who had the most interest and pride in Forty Acres, and it broke his heart to see it remaining empty most of the time after his grandparents' deaths. So with his brothers he formed a foundation in order to preserve the estate as a museum. As its charms are now displayed, so are its countless relics from all the old families whose lines have joined the procession through the house. Practically every item in it is a century old, and some of them are as much as 175 years of age.

Even the first Elizabeth's spinning wheel is there, in the north kitchen, although the sound of its whirring often comes from the attic. Children in the family were told it was only squirrels or a cat playing, but the adults always knew better. Eventually they apparently gave up trying to fool anybody, and came right out with the fact that they had a ghost in the house. But this was many years later.

Dr. Huntington is not in the least reluctant to speak about it. He says, "We have no idea when the countryside began to think of the house as haunted. No one in the family seemed to be aware of ghostly presences until my father's generation was growing up. But they heard, as members of my generation and the next have, a firm, light step coming up the stairs to the third-floor attic after midnight, sometimes as late as sunrise, a step so definite that whoever hears it can never forget the sound. The door from the second-floor hall to this stair could be firmly closed and latched at night and yet found open in the morning.

"My youngest brother, sleeping in the attic bedroom, heard the approaching step come up on two successive nights and on the third, he rushed down the stairs, passing something or someone about the height of a child, on the way down. He spent the rest of that night on a sofa in the Long Room and would never sleep in that attic room again.

"I have seen, in the moonlight or the small hours of the morning, a latch rise and a door open. I have also been perfectly aware of a presence in an adjoining room and going in expectantly found no one. Visitors sitting with the family in the Long Room or at the dining room table have asked, 'Who was that who just went past the door?' They have had an impression of someone unfamiliar hurrying by, although no one knew who it could be."

Dr. Huntington mentions a certain high, sustained musical note that vibrates now and then, by day as well as by night. He adds also, "Some of us children waked at night to find a figure bending over the bed, someone whose full skirt of oddly patterned design and frilled white cap were perfectly visible in the dark."

"Don't mind that," his aunts would say. "We have all seen her." Indeed, it was so taken as a matter of course that when one of the children sometimes happened to mention to his mother, "I felt you come and tuck me in last night," she would reply, "No, that must have been the ghost."

It is strange, isn't it, that no one spoke of her until these latter generations? Did people just refuse to acknowledge her presence before that time, even though they were aware of it? Or has she only started manifesting some hundred years or so after her death? Or might the entity be not an Elizabeth after all but someone who died more recently?

Well, no matter who she is or when she started making herself known, I strongly suspect that she is still there, even though the chatter of adults is no longer stilled suddenly to hear her spinning, and there are no children living in the house for her to tuck into bed. I can't say I have *seen* her, but there was something unexplainable in my experience in the house.

I always make an attempt to gain personal impressions in the ghost houses I visit. I learn as little as possible about the building before going in, and then record what I feel in the various rooms. After that I ask which rooms are supposed to be the most haunted, and where certain manifestations are alleged to have taken place. In most of the houses visited in my research for this book, I have had little or no reaction. I have already mentioned the house where delicious chills ran up my spine; and in one or two I felt slightly depressed. But nowhere have I seen anything unusual. Because my responses have been so negative on the whole, perhaps the two slight experiences I had in the Bishop Huntington House may be worth some mention.

About eleven o'clock one beautiful summer morning the caretaker's wife took me through the house privately, and we were accompanied by her black cocker spaniel, Annie.

"Are you sure the presence of a dog won't keep the ghost from manifesting?" I asked her. "I mean, if there's any chance of her making an appearance, we want to have everything as receptive as possible." No matter how many dogs are supposed to have reacted positively to ghosts, my personal feeling is that a pet clomping and sniffling around would be likely to cover up any faint phantom rustlings, should they occur. But the lady did not take the hint and Annie remained. I tried again. "Has Annie ever seen anything peculiar in this house?" I asked.

"No," I was told calmly, "she hasn't, and I haven't either."

With Annie at our heels, we went into the house by the front door and turned right and walked into the northeast downstairs bedroom where the sword had been passed through the window. There was the little four-poster bed on which the impressions had so often been seen. Now its counterpane was as smooth as a competent housekeeper could make it. I wished aloud that I could have seen the dents and taken a picture of them such as appeared in a popular weekly magazine several years ago. The caretaker assured me that there had not been any dents on the bed that day, either. She said she strongly suspected that the photographer had herself made the ones which were so evident in her picture.

Just then I happened to glance into the hall and saw a shadow cross the sunlight coming through the two long narrow windows flanking the front door. At the same moment Annie, who was sitting on the floor in front of the bed, perked up her ears and got a bright, expectant look on her face.

"Somebody's coming," I said, taking it as a matter of course.

"No," said the caretaker's wife, who, while very pleasant, was also very sure of herself about the old house and its activities, "we're alone here."

I was not convinced and walked to the front door and looked out. She was right. No one was there. And visibility was so clear all around the house and grounds that no one could have been there and disappeared before I arrived at the door. I looked back at the sunlight in the hall to see if the movement of trees outside could have cast such a shadow, but it did not seem in any way likely. Annie relaxed again, and so did I. Obviously we had made a mistake.

Later, I was left alone on the second floor of the house for a while. I had examined the queer old brick smoke oven which had once been used to cure the meat; then I turned and walked down the hall. I was heading toward a narrow door which opened onto a steep flight of steps going up into the attic. Just as I arrived at the foot of the stairs and looked up I saw an extremely vague grayishness at the top of the steps on the left. It was like a quick flick of mist, hardly enough even to speak of, and yet it was definite, and in a place where there could be no reflection of any sort. It was the first thing of this nature I had ever seen in my life; and it *was* in that attic, which I later learned was one of the favorite haunts of Elizabeth. Right below the spot where I saw the swish of gossamer gray is the famous door from this back hall into the front hall, whose iron latch has the tradition of opening by itself.

As Dr. Huntington says in his book, "None of these manifestations are actually very startling, but even without twilight or midnight to help the imagination, in bright sunshine, the sense of the unseen can often seem too much and too near."

CHAPTER SEVEN

HAWAIIAN HAUNTS

NEVER MISTREAT A STRANGE OLD WOMAN IN HAWAII. She may be Madame Pele and give you a rough time if you do. And if a beautiful young girl disappears in front of your eyes, you are really in for trouble. Whenever Pele, in any of the various embodiments in which she appears, feels slighted, she retaliates quickly, and very unpleasantly, by causing Mauna Loa to erupt. She can do it, you see, because she is the goddess of the volcano.

Some people will tell you that it is only in primitive areas of the islands that Madame Pele still makes her appearances; but even those sophisticated moderns who maintain this are very tactful with strange old women. And they handle beautiful young girls as if they were china dolls.

A person who sits in a comfortable armchair in New York City, or Atlanta, or Bismarck, North Dakota, and reads about the ghostly appearances of native Hawaiian gods may shrug them off as myth. A casual visitor to Honolulu may sneer at the idea of taking local superstitions seriously. Admittedly, much of this city looks like Miami Beach at its most glittering, since tourists from the mainland are its chief source of revenue. This is not the real Hawaii, as anyone who is at all perceptive will realize. Yet it is possible to visit Honolulu and leave without ever going below its surface and without realizing the genuine warmth and graciousness of the natives.

To get the "feel" of these glamorous islands, so that it will be easier for you to understand how the real Hawaiians still believe in their folklore and traditions, which are as much a part of their lives as the fantastic flowers and the abundant tropical foliage, picture yourself in a Honolulu park. Sitting under the wide spread of a monkey pod tree, or amidst the tangled roots of a banyan, watch the little courting doves bowing to each other and reiterating their pleasantly monotonous "koo-*koos*." The languorous loveliness will soon engulf you; you will wish to continue to sit there indefinitely, completely satisfied about the state of your existence.

But now that you have been introduced to the charms of Oahu, you should go to the other islands, which are even more captivating because less overrun with tourists. Since it is all a mental projection, it won't even cost you plane fare. I want you to get to know the people who live on Kauai, or Maui, or the Big Island (Hawaii). Almost anyone you meet there with dark skin or slanting eyes is, while part other Polynesian races or part Japanese, also probably some fraction native Hawaiian. Many of the white-skinned individuals have lived long on the islands and intermarried with other ethnic groups. These peoples are the most truly amalgamated of any in the world, and what belongs to the original natives has been acquired to some degree by everyone.

Naturally these island dwellers will not discuss their cherished beliefs with strangers; but if you warm them with your enthusiasm and your genuine interest in their traditions, you will eventually begin to hear things that may surprise you. Even those who pretend not to believe seriously in the stories they relate will tell them with more than casual interest. And when they speak about the Night Marchers, they will speak very delicately and very quietly, because everyone knows someone who has actually seen these ghostly processions.

You will be told with a laugh about the Menehunes—the mythical dwarfs with superhuman strength who are the legendary little people of the islands similar to the leprechauns of Ireland. Stories are frequent about how they have done prodigious and helpful tasks at night; but they must always complete their work before the first fingers of light search through the green mountains.

Of all the historical gods of Hawaii, Madame Pele is the one you will hear the most about. But don't take her too lightly just because people tease about her. Everybody on the Big Island knows from experience that soon after reports begin to come in that she has been sighted, the volcano will erupt. As the Honolulu *Star-Bulletin* headlined on July 22, 1956: "Be Kind to Madame Pele or Face the Results."

Pele comes from a distinctive family of gods, the seven Hiiake sisters. She is a capricious, haughty, beautiful woman who demands reverence. That is why she must be called Madame. It is said that her first home was off the Island of Kauai, and from there she roamed through the other islands and finally arrived at the Big Island. When she got there she began to dig, day and night, and finally came to fire. This was the warm hearth for which she had been searching; and the Kilauea Crater on the side of Mauna Loa is now known officially as the home of Madame Pele.

These are some of the tales about the fire goddess.

There was once a large fish pond three miles long at Paaica on the Kona Coast of the Island of Hawaii. One day an old woman appeared and asked a group of busy fishermen for some fish or shrimps; but they refused her. The white-haired hag turned and left. But that night the people living on the beach saw a fire on the volcanic peak called Hualalai. Gradually, as it came closer, they realized that the red flame against the dark was a molten river of lava. They then knew that the old woman the fishermen had rejected was Pele. The fish pond of Paaica was reached by the lava. It rushed into the still, cool water, and with a great hiss, and clouds of steam, the water evaporated. The pond was no more.

Another story concerns two girls from a village on the western slope of Hualalai. Their families both lived in separate ends of the same house. When an old lady came up to the two girls as they were roasting breadfruit, one girl shared some with her and the other did not. The old woman told the generous girl to have her parents mark their door that night. When the girl related this to her parents, they knew she must have seen Pele, and they hastened to put a tapa leaf on their door. That night there were no warnings of earthquake or thunder, and unsuspecting villagers slept peacefully. But a thin, slow stream of lava moved toward the sea. It became wider and spread over the countryside as it went; when it reached the village, it overran the end of the house where the girl who had refused to share her breadfruit lay sleeping. The other end of the house was untouched.

As you drive through the vast desolate areas on the Big Island, which are covered by black cinders and lava rocks, you can't help wondering at such tales, even though they sound like myths. Something makes the flow go in one direction rather than another. What is it?

There are a few occasions when the lava flow has been diverted by supplications to Pele. Once during an eruption a big flow was heading directly toward the lovely city of Hilo. The Princess Ruth, a sister of the great Hawaiian King Kamehameha, with eight of her suitors, went out to try to protect the city, while all its inhabitants prayed. Ruth stood near the cascading flames and molten lava and plucked a chicken. Then with proper ceremony she tossed it into the lava flow for Madame Pele. No one was surprised, and all were fantastically gratified, when the flow immediately diverted around the town.

A similar instance occurred as recently as 1960 at Kapoho, where a lighthouse stood in the direct path of the lava flow. People in the lighthouse prayed frantically to Madame Pele as the flaming mass poured down the mountain, heading directly toward them. Just before it reached the lighthouse it diverted, and flowed around it and rushed into the sea. A look at a local map shows how the 1960 lava flow at Kapoho divided and spared the lighthouse, even though it destroyed everything else in the area.

It is said, incidentally, that when the lava hits the ocean you can see, it you watch carefully, the profile of Madame Pele in the cloud formations.

A beautiful woman in a red dress has been reported acting mysteriously at Hilton's Hawaiian Village Hotel on occasion. *Really* mysteriously: she disappears in front of your eyes. *The Sunday Advertiser* stated on August 16, 1959, that a "woman of unearthly beauty asked for help in finding a room number at the hotel. She disappeared while walking beside an employee toward the room. Pele does that sort of thing." There are other reports of ghosts of various kinds at the Hawaiian Village, allegedly seen by employees and long-time residents alike. These are not necessarily goddess-type ghosts like Pele, but are said to involve a well-suppressed story of a murder once committed in a secret room high up in a tower. Of course, upper echelon hotel personnel tend to discount these stories quickly and emphatically.

Pele does not always appear as a woman before an eruption. Sometimes she just causes strange lights and other phenomena. There was much in the newspapers about odd goings-on on the Saddle Road near Hilo shortly before the 1955 eruption of Kilauea. It started in the early morning hours of January 31 when the Henry Macomber family encountered a powerful force that rocked their truck back and forth in a manner no wind could have. Then they saw unexplained lights on the highway, when there were no cars or people about.

A group of government officials encountered the identical lights during the same week that the Macombers saw them. And Pedro Monzano, a taxi driver, had his tire wrench tossed at his feet while he was putting a tire on his taxi alone on the Saddle Road. He looked all around and no one was there, yet his wrench had been lifted from the trunk of his car and deposited at his feet. Monzano tightened the lugs on his tire as quickly as he could and sped away, without even taking time to affix his hub cap.

After such reports no one was surprised when the volcano erupted within a short time.

One of the more interesting events involving the fire goddess is her spectacular defiance by the high chieftess Kapiolani. Born a pagan, Kapiolani lived through the taboo period, and after the missionaries arrived she became a Christian. In December 1824, she determined to overcome the Hawaiians' deep fear of Pele. Accompanied by a few followers, she journeyed to the rim of Kilauea, and ate the sacrificial foods. But then she stood up and declaimed loudly: "I fear not Pele. If I perish in her anger, then you may fear Pele; but if I trust in Jehovah, then you must fear and serve Him alone."

Her followers knelt in prayer, and no harm came to Kapiolani as a result of this defiant action. But why did Pele let her get away with it? Perhaps she admired her courage. Although Pele probably would be more likely to agree with the sentiments expressed by George Nawoakoa, who says, "I sometimes think that our people were better Christians before the missionaries came."

George Nawoakoa is one who has seen the phantom Night Travelers and lived to tell the tale, and he told it to Antoinette Withington. She repeated it in "Ghostly Processions in Hawaii" (*Harper's Monthly Magazine,* May 1937). George says, "The time that I saw it, I was coming home along the road. I had been to a neighbor's. It was getting toward dark. There was a little new moon but it did not affect the darkness. As I said, I was walking along alone when suddenly I saw something strange ahead of me, coming toward me. It seemed like a cloud of dust, but it shone like silver. It was then that I looked at the moon and knew that it was not that which made the shining. When I looked longer it seemed to me that it was smoke—and just then I saw the dead people and I knew it must be a procession. I had heard that if the people in the procession caught sight of a living person that person might drop dead or the procession would disappear instantly. I crouched down by a big stone along the side of the road and they did not see me. There were old people and young ones and all sorts. Some of them were singing in a sort of way—it didn't sound just like singing—I couldn't tell. . . .

"They were quite a time going by. My young cousin had died a year before and I looked to see if she might not be with them, but I didn't see anyone I knew. They were all so white and strange. But they went right on to the old *heiau* [temple] and I heard the drums beating."

"Drums?" ventured Antoinette Withington.

"Yes, and we sometimes hear them now."

A young woman told Miss Withington: "You know, I was educated on the mainland and I did not believe many things which our Hawaiian people believe." However, a well-known physician, a Caucasian, who used to tell of having seen the mysterious procession of the walking ghosts, persuaded her to go with him on one of the nights of Kane (a certain time of the moon), when he thought the spirits might be walking. He took her to a hillside not far from an old temple and there they waited. Hours went by; midnight came but no spirits came with it. The couple was about to give up and go home when suddenly the doctor said, "Wait! Be still! They are coming!"

"I was amazed," the young woman related, "to see a long line of people slowly moving up from the water and steadily climbing the hill. They appeared strange, and as though touched with a shimmering radiance. Each figure carried a light. I could almost see their faces through the darkness. They were chanting in old Hawaiian as they moved on up to the *heiau*—and then we heard the drums. I was never so terrified in my life. My knees shook under me and I had to sit down on the ground and pull myself together. Never again will I say that I do not believe what I have been told about these sacred things."

So now you can see why, if a native Hawaiian hears distant drums during the nights of Kane, he hides quickly. Joseph Kauanui of Anahole, on the Island of Kauai, saw the Night Marchers when he was about eight years old, too young to know he must hide. Fortunately his uncle was with him. Joseph's wife Blossom Kauanui

drives a limousine and acts as guide for the Grey Lines, and she
and I were alone as we returned from a tour of the island. I
asked her casually if she had ever seen the Night Travelers and
expected a shrug, or a turn of the conversation to other subjects;
but instead she told me with no hesitation of her husband's personal
experience. He and his uncle were riding on a horse one beautiful
tropical night when they heard a whispering sound as if many
people were coming at a distance. Then they felt an unusual wind
blowing. Joseph's uncle knew the portent of these sounds, and he
got off his horse quickly and pulled the boy down behind a rock.
Then they peeped out and watched the most unusual sight of their
lives. First they heard voices, and they could distinguish the actual
language being spoken. Then they saw what looked like a wavering
mist coming toward them. As the procession passed, the wind blew
strongly. Joseph's uncle identified the voice of a deceased relative
in the throng of spirits who marched past them; but the boy himself
was too young to be sure of anything except that he was scared
to death.

John Dominis Holt is a tall, pleasant man who is an excellent
example of a bicultural combination of races in the islands. He is a
landscape architect by profession and lives on the Island of Oahu.
His skin is as white as any suntanned Caucasian, and he speaks
with a British accent, but he is related to some of the most important
Hawaiians, among them a great-uncle who was Queen Liliuokalani's
husband. He is also descended from the early missionaries. Quite
naturally proud of his ancestry, Holt combines in his makeup the
mystical and spiritual heritage of the natives and the culture of a
well-reared modern gentleman.

John Dominis Holt spoke to me quite freely about the island
ghosts. He has had personal experience with them. One story of
interest is about what happened when he was a boy and lived
part of the time on the west coast of Oahu near Kawela Bay.
He says, "My father had gone fishing with a great-uncle of mine,
a dilettante fisherman with vast yards of nets and a fishing crew.
Mother was at home with a nurse to take care of her children—
three at that time—and a Chinese handyman, Ah Ling, and Boboda,
a pure Hawaiian who acted as gardener." Holt's mother was psychic;
and sometime during the evening, after his father had gone fishing,
she had a premonition that something was wrong.

Holt says: "She had Ah Ling hitch up the buggy. It was during the late 1920s and buggies were out of style, but we still used them at the beach. We all piled into it and drove down one of the narrow, sandy lanes. The ironwood trees were howling in the wind, and Mother was getting more and more frightened. We had driven about half a mile away from the house and were in a region called Waiale'e when the horse reared up, frightened by something which we could not see. My mother was convinced that it was a spirit. The Chinese cook in absolute terror leaped out of the buggy and ran back toward the house. Mother took the reins and tried to get the horse to move. He kept rearing up instead."

The desperate mother managed to get the horse across the spot in the road which had so bothered him, but the path was blocked down below by a fallen tree. In a panic, she turned the buggy around to go back toward the house. But, Holt says, "When we came to the spot again the horse stopped, neighed, and reared up. Mother then took another lane and went out to the main road which was macadamized—not good for horses, of course. But she managed to get by the spot on this road and down to the beach where my father and great-uncle were nipping heavily on Okolehao, the native Hawaiian equivalent of bathtub gin and infinitely better."

When his mother described what had happened, "Uncle William said that we had driven into the path of the spirits and that they were in a procession going to the sea and we had tried to cross the line of their procession." He added, "These could either have been the Marchers of the Night or an ancient funeral procession going up to the cliffs from the sea."

"The whole coastline is alive with spirit life," concludes John Dominis Holt. Who are we to dispute him?

CHAPTER EIGHT

A GHOST NAMED SMITH

IT HARDLY SEEMS LIKELY THAT IN ALL OF AMERICA there should not be a single well-known ghost name Smith, and I think I've found one—a little old lady spirit who must be a descendant of Governor Samuel E. Smith of Maine.

The Lee Payson Smith house where she lives is on High Street, at the top of the common in Wiscasset, which calls itself Maine's prettiest village. There is a special reason that Wiscasset can say this about itself and get away with it—the spectacular charm of its streets lined with tall elm trees and commanding white mansions. The Smith house is one of the nicest of the old homes in Wiscasset, and would be famous even if it did not have a ghost, because of the beauty of its construction. Not large as colonial mansions go, the house is elegant in detail. It was erected in 1792 by the Honorable Silas Lee, a lawyer who apparently spared no expense in constructing a building that is said to be one of the finest examples of early American architecture in Maine. Even today artists and architects make summer pilgrimages to sketch its mullioned windows, and particularly its semicircular portico whose entablature is supported by Ionic columns. Inside, the house has the same fine detail of construction; plus two large portraits of Governor Smith and his wife; and a little old ghost who sits and rocks in her favorite mahogany rocking chair because she just will not leave the house she loved so much.

In 1807 Silas Lee sold his home to General David Payson, from whose heirs it was purchased by Governor Smith in 1836, and it has belonged to Smiths ever since. It is now in the joint possession of the Governor's great-granddaughter, Marion (Mrs. Lloyd)

Lowndes, and her sister-in-law, Tanya, the widow of Emerson Smith. This came about when Mrs. Lowndes's mother, the author Susan Grant Smith (no relation to the author of this book) willed the house to both her son and her daughter. The present owners live in it in alternating years, and in early summer it is sometimes unoccupied before one family or the other arrives for the season.

It was during such a period that Robert Miller saw the ghost. Robert works at the Musical Wonder House, another architectural showplace, which is right next door to the Smith house. Robert is the nice-looking, slender young man who greets you at the door when you go in to see the curious music boxes and other mechanical instruments on exhibit there. He is also a young man who sees ghosts. But he hardly expected to see one on May 25, 1966, when he was working, about eight o'clock in the evening, in the upstairs front bedroom of the Music House.

"I was painting and papering up there getting ready to open for the season," Robert says. "I happened to look out the window and saw the old lady next door standing at the window wearing a bonnet that stood out around her face and a full black skirt. She had a white frilly thing at her throat." Since the Smith house was unoccupied at the time, he was "really shook."

Robert Miller had known about the ghost before, although he was not sure he believed in it until he saw it himself. Marion Lowndes's daughter Susan had told him that she had seen the famous chair rocking when no one visible was in it. He had heard that Mrs. Susan Smith, too, had evidence of the ghost, hearing footsteps and other sounds coming from closed and locked rooms. Other occupants of the house before her had reported similar disturbances.

One woman who lived there once walked into the front drawing room in which the chair sits by the window, and found the little old lady quietly rocking. As she started to greet her, the figure disappeared. No one could convince this tenant that she had been "seeing things." Robert Miller is the same way. He gets lots of teasing about his ghosts, but he is *sure*.

One breezy August afternoon Susan Smith and her sister, Mary Grant Rafter, were sitting in the hedge-enclosed formal garden back of the house, when Mrs. Rafter looked up at the library window and said, "Now, who's that?"

"Who do you mean?" asked Mrs. Smith. "There's no one in the house."

"Yes, there is," Mrs. Rafter insisted. "I just saw her, didn't you? Looking out that window. A woman with a long nose and a little white cap on her head. Oh, of course, it must be the ghost."

The woman who haunts the house lived in it about a hundred years ago, and she had so much unhappiness that she never seems to have gotten over it. Marion Lowndes has written a beautiful story about her home called "The Well Loved House" in her book *Ghosts that Still Walk,* and she describes the life of the haunt with warmth and color. She says that "through the bitter winters and the unadventurous summers" she kept house ably and grimly for her husband and her five sons. "She had no imagination or spirit to soften her life, but she did have endurance."

However, even stolid endurance is not enough when Fate begins to manhandle a family. Tragedy struck them all in turn. The youngest son was lost at sea off India, another was killed in the Civil War, a third died of drink, and another of pneumonia. The last son became a recluse, secluding himself in the one-story north wing of the house and living there until the end of his life without speaking to anyone—alone with his law books and his black-and-white setter named Guy. This man is referred to as "Jasper," although the records do not contain his name or the names of any of his brothers; but there is a family tradition that "Uncle Jasper's spirit" hangs around that area. The wing in which he secluded himself has since burned down, but the door that opened into that part of the house remains. And often the big dog is still heard leaping against that door and scratching to get into the house.

To complete the tragic cycle, the old lady's husband, once an able and distinguished man, ended his days as a fretful invalid in a wing chair. All this would be enough to embitter anyone, unless she had an unusually reassuring religious belief or a philosophy which made her hard life supportable. All this woman had was her house. It may have been enough. Marion Lowndes says:

"The old lady looked round her beautiful lifeless rooms—at her carved cornices and her elegant mahoganies and her gold wallpaper shining in the candlelight. Outside she heard the yellow elm branches lashing in the line gale and she felt how the storm spent itself against her long Greek façade, indifferent and serene in its classic perfection.

" 'Everything else has failed me,' she said when she was dying, 'except this house. If I can, I'll come back.'

"She loved the house, like everyone else who has lived there," Mrs. Lowndes says, ". . . and no one, now, ever feels alone there."

But there was a time when people wished they were alone— for whoever was in there with them was making an unholy nuisance of herself. About fifty years ago things got so bad that people used to walk on the other side of the street when passing the house. The owners were in Europe at the time, and the house had been rented to a Captain and Mrs. Babson. They had placed all the Smiths' personal possessions in the south drawing room for storage and locked the doors. But almost as soon as they moved in they heard sounds coming from this closed room. The wind seemed to whistle through there, although it did so nowhere else in the house. Occasionally the noise of someone prowling around that room disturbed the Babsons; but if they went to the keyhole and listened, the sounds stopped. Then crashes, and loud reports like pistol shots, began to occur frequently. Finally, in an effort to secure peace, they opened the room. They found it intact, except that the two family portraits of note—Governor and Mrs. Smith— had been disarranged. These were restored to their proper places, facing each other on the walls, and the doors were left open. Immediately all disturbances ceased. But people still passed the house on the opposite side of the road.

Mrs. Lowndes tells a story about her mother's experience with a group of friends, as it was relayed to her by one of them named Hoffman. Mrs. Smith had just returned to the house from New York to reopen it, and Mr. Hoffman and several others had dropped in on her for supper. They thoughtfully had brought along the gleanings from their own refrigerators as they knew that she had not had time to bring in any groceries. The meal turned out to be a very filling and a very friendly one. They ate before the fire in the drawing room—that same south parlor of previous renown— because the furnace had not been started. All the doors were closed and the diners had drawn close to the open fire for warmth. Hoffman said:

"The candles were flickering and one or two of them had gone out. Most of the light there was came from the fire which had been well fed too—with crackling, pungent birch. The table had been cleared and put away so that we could draw closer to its welcome warmth. The Smiths' old poodle had obligingly sprawled on the hearth and gone sound asleep, making a perfect fender to rest our toes against.

"And then in the midst of our talk—animated talk, too, it was, not the late, lazy, just-before-you-ease-yourself-up-and-leave variety —it happened. . . .

"I can only call it enchantment, what happened to us in the middle of that sentence that 'it' interrupted. For instead of freezing us into alertness it spellbound us—as if we were dreaming this all of a sudden. We just sat there caught in a thick, syrupy mood that made us keep quiet and only stare into the fire.

"All except the dog, that is. He had come fully awake and was pricking his long curly ears. And his brown eyes rolled in his head with fright and confusion. . . .

"But if I couldn't move or speak, I could hear. There were footsteps—slow, deliberate, like those of a person who is very old. They were coming down the uncarpeted stairs outside in the hall— beyond that closed door which I could just see out of the corner of one eye.

"On and on they came until I thought I should choke for not being able to speak to the others, to startle them into some slight movement at least, and ask, 'What is it?' or, 'Do you hear it too?'

"And then at last they were at the bottom. A pause. And they came on straight for the drawing room!

"With a great effort—again like in a dream, when you're running away from something and can't make any headway—or maybe like the movement in a slow-motion film—I managed to turn my head and look at the door into the hall.

"It opened . . . and there was nothing there."

Mr. Hoffman concluded that he believed the house was haunted, and that he would always continue to believe that it was haunted. And I will, too. By a little old lady named Smith.

CHAPTER NINE

GENEVIEVE, ST. GENEVIEVE

JULES VALLE SAID TO HIS WIFE Anne-Marie one morning, "I almost called out to you last night, dear. I thought you came in and touched me on the shoulder."

"No, I didn't," she answered. "I slept through the night."

"I know you didn't," her husband said. "It was three little old men."

"It was *what?*"

"Three old men. They ended at the waist, so they must have been ghosts. They wore old-fashioned clothes."

There are some people, you know, who are not terribly surprised when ghosts stop by their beds at night for a visit. Mr. Valle seems to have been one of these. He was a prominent businessman from St. Louis who had recently bought a small old house in St. Genevieve, a little town about sixty miles down the Mississippi. Perhaps he just took it for granted that haunts came with it. He and his wife had retired to this house at 1 North Street in the town where he had kinsmen. They had remodeled and redecorated it, and then Mr. Valle had to have an operation for the removal of an eye. A boxing injury, incurred when he was a young man, had grown increasingly troublesome, and the doctors insisted that surgery was necessary. He saw the ghosts while he was convalescing.

When the three phantoms appeared, standing beside his bed looking down at him, Mr. Valle was curious about why they had come. He realized that they must be ghosts, but he wondered why ghosts should come to visit him. Fortunately they were all smiling and nodding to him pleasantly, so he knew they must have some good purpose in mind. Even after they faded away, he kept lying there in his bed wondering what the purpose of their visit might have been. He finally decided they must have been there to encourage him about his operation; and it is true, he did get completely well again, living for ten years afterward.

His wife, knowing about those ghosts and others that have been evident from time to time in the house, has nonetheless remained there alone since her husband's death. She is a tiny woman, attractive and pleasantly plump. And she is exceedingly spunky, for she, too, has had experience with the haunts in her home.

This house is undoubtedly the most exquisite ghost house in America, not only in its original interesting construction and beautiful paint and wallpaper, but in the lovely and tasteful antiques with which it is furnished. Its history is interwoven with the history of St. Genevieve, which was settled in 1735 by the French. Later the Spanish held St. Genevieve for some years, and then it went back into French hands again for a while before it was acquired by the United States.

Who built the house is not known. Its earliest historical owner was Jacques Dubreuil Guibourd. Born in France, Guibourd went to the French side of Santo Domingo, which is now Haiti, when he was a young man. In the great Negro uprising of the late 1700s his life was in danger, and he was saved by a slave named Moro. The means of his escape from the island was a large keg in which he was hidden while Moro carried it on board a ship bound for Philadelphia. Arriving in that port, Guibourd soon met some fellow Frenchmen, with whom he could communicate.

It was the custom at that time for the merchants of St. Genevieve, Missouri, to go on horseback all the way to Philadelphia to buy their supplies. It was these men whom Guibourd met, and he decided to accompany them back to their home. In St. Genevieve he bought the little house—Valle's little house—and soon was married and settled down. His wife was Ursule Barbeau, daughter of the Commandant at Prarie de Roche, the fort across the river, and Jules Valle's great-grandfather's sister.

One of Guibourd's descendants whom the Valles well remember was Miss Victorine, whom everyone called Miss Vickie. She died in the bedroom now occupied by Mrs. Valle. One of Miss Vickie's brothers, a doctor, committed suicide in the house after a bank failure. It is not known who the three men in old-fashioned clothes might have been, but in a place so old, they could have been most anybody.

Mrs. Elizabeth Heins, a close friend of Anne-Marie's, and "a born medium," came to visit shortly after the Valles moved into the house. She knew, of course, of its French background. Yet one of the first things she said after she had looked around was, "Yes, but there was Spanish spoken in this house, too." The Valles did not know what that meant, for at that time they had learned very little about the actual background of their home. But Jules later met a man well-versed in the history of the town who told him that, during the Spanish occupation of St. Genevieve, 1 North Street had been the social headquarters for the Spanish officers, who went there to be entertained.

"We did know that St. Genevieve had been under the Spanish flag and that there had been a garrison in the town for a time," Anne-Marie says, "but we did not know they had used our house."

Mrs. Valle has only heard the ghosts, even though her husband saw some of them. But she is not the only one who has heard them. She says: "I had an old colored maid of whom I was fond, Dora Williams. After she died I had a succession of maids who declared that they heard Dora's footsteps."

The kitchen of the house is in a little back wing which used to be the slaves' quarters. The room and bath that the maids use is upstairs over the kitchen and dining room, and it is there that the footsteps are heard. "Dora was devoted to me, and awfully jealous," Mrs. Valle says. "I have only heard her once walk across the floor, but others have heard her often." In order to dispel the thought that this might merely be floor boards creaking from natural causes, Mrs. Valle says, "There never were any such sounds before Dora's death. They have only occurred since then."

Dogs have been quite aware of the supernatural in this house, although just what they have experienced cannot be determined. The current canine occupant is a huge one-year-old collie named Jamie, who delights in bounding on everybody. Twice Jamie has seemed to be conscious of another dog in the house. He has stood at the living room door and growled, with his tail hanging down, but wagging. The quiet growl is the sound he uses when meeting strange dogs. He is not frightened, but he is definitely registering a specific emotion. On both occasions, Mrs. Valle verified that there was nothing outside which would have caused his reaction. Indeed,

Jamie was making no effort to go out. She believes instead that he had in some way briefly seen one of the previous dog occupants of the house. There are two of which she knows because they were hers.

Her Scottie named Dusky used also to see things in the house, but they would frighten him almost crazy until he got outside. He would be cowering, abject, almost anguished as he attempted to get out of the house on those certain occasions. Anne-Marie never found out what had caused those sudden spells of his, unless he, too, was seeing phantoms.

Mrs. Valle also had another collie, Peter, who died in the house. She thinks Jamie may have seen him. It was when a friend named Helene was visiting her that Jamie had one of his meetings with his invisible companion. Helene had been unusually fond of the collie, Peter, and he of her. Mrs. Valle suggests that Peter, from his place in the hereafter, visited her at the time she had Helene as a house guest. And she believes that Jamie sensed his presence. She is glad that Helene also saw Jamie's curious act, if for no other reason than to back her up when she tells of something so difficult to understand.

Anne-Marie is also happy that she stood her ground with the ghosts who were most unpleasant to her. Mr. Valle had died in January 1949, and one night about the middle of March of that year she awoke to hear dreadful noises coming from his room— as if the place were being torn apart. It sounded as if the furniture were being thrown about and broken, as if pictures and lamps were being smashed. There were no voices, only this incredible din. She knew at once that this was no robbery—for what robbers would be so noisy? Anyway, the house was securely closed and locked and no one could possibly have gotten in. To her mind there was no other explanation than a poltergeist type of ghost—those noisy and vicious invisible racketers who make life miserable for the people upon whom they occasionally perpetrate their unpleasant pranks.

As the noise continued for perhaps ten or fifteen minutes, Mrs. Valle got incredibly angry.

"I have a terrible temper," she told me, "and when it is aroused I'm not afraid of the devil." Coming from a woman who declares herself to be too timid to drive a car, and who looks like a doll, this is a surprising statement. But it must be true—for that night, when she became absolutely furious, she *turned her back* on the poltergeists. She sat up in bed and declared very loudly, "Whoever or whatever you are, listen to me! You are *not* going to run me out of my house. Do you hear me? You are not going to frighten me from my home." Then she lay back down, pulled the covers up to her chin, rolled over, and went to sleep.

The next morning as soon as she awoke she went into her husband's room and found that not one thing had been touched or moved. She realized that her stubborn resistance, as she calls it —although some might term it bravery beyond the call of duty—had accomplished what she had intended.

"If I'd given in and become frightened," she says, "I'm sure they would have started a real poltergeist parade in here."

Perhaps she is right. Who knows, when ghosts are involved?

CHAPTER TEN

THE GENERAL
AND THE DEVIL

A MAN MAY BECOME A LEGEND IN HIS OWN TIME; or he may become one after he dies, especially if he is reputed to be a ghost. Not many men have the privilege, if it may so be called, of being a legend both before and after their deaths. General Jonathan Moulton of Hampton, New Hampshire, has this distinction—to such an extent that it is completely impossible to clarify where the fiction about him ends and the truth begins.

The folklore probably starts with his selling his soul to the devil, although some of his contemporaries would have sworn that this was a truth beyond question. In fact, they did swear it.

The solid, incontrovertible facts begin with his birth. He was a real flesh and blood man, who was born July 21, 1726, and died September 18, 1787. He was first married on February 22, 1749, to Abigail, the daughter of Benjamin Smith. He was married a second time on September 11, 1776, to Sarah, daughter of Dr. Anthony Emery. His war record was probably authentic also, for he rose to the rank of general in the French and Indian Wars, where he acquired considerable celebrity as an Indian fighter. Samuel Adams Drake says in *New England Legends and Folklore* that Moulton's passion was to exterminate the Abenaki warriors and conjurers, among whom he had lived.

From here on we are on our own about General Jonathan Moulton. Practically anything else that can be learned about him can be taken or left alone; but we'd best be on our guard. Apparently it was after he was married and had a home of his own that he said to Abigail one day, "I've got to get hold of some money. I am not a man ever to be satisfied with a retired army general's pension. I need cash, wealth, riches, money to burn."

There is not much doubt that Abigail agreed with him. What woman wouldn't?

"I'd sell my soul for unbounded wealth," the general went on. But here he lost Abigail, who was a rather conservative type. One day not long after this rash statement was made, he was standing alone by the fireside when a shower of sparks came down the chimney and out stepped a man dressed from top to toe in black velvet. His ruffles were not even smutted. Moulton was immediately alert, for this sort of thing did not happen often in his circles. Obviously his offer to sell his soul had been heard at headquarters. He played it cool. He took out his jackknife and began to whittle. He had often said that neither man nor devil could get the better of him in a trade, and he was about to prove it.

The devil, for indeed it was he, took out his jackknife also, and began to pare his nails. After a while they started to dicker, and finally they made a deal that the devil was to make the general the richest man in the province. An actual text of the devil's compact was published in Drake's book. It reads: "In consideration of one agreement, duly signed and sealed, to deliver your soul, I engage on my part, on the first day of every month, to fill your boots with golden guineas. But mark well, if you try to play me any tricks, you will repent it. I know you, Jonathan Moulton, and shall keep my eye upon you; so beware!" This was duly signed by both parties and filed away somewhere for safekeeping.

After that, every month the golden guineas dropped into the boots. "It is true," Drake states, "that Moulton ransacked the village for the largest pair of boots to be found, and had finally secured a brace of trooper's jack boots which came nearly to his thighs. But the devil does not stand upon trifles." Soon Jonathan Moulton began to roll in wealth. Everything he touched prospered. He could do no wrong financially. His neighbors regarded him first with envy; but as time went on their reaction was one of repugnance, and ultimately their main emotion regarding him was fear.

A man can be too greedy even for the devil. And one day when Lucifer came to fill Moulton's boots with lucre he found himself unable to do so. It was like putting water down a rat hole. He poured golden guineas and more golden guineas into the boots, but they never filled up. So he decided to take a look and see what was amiss. He discovered that Moulton had cut the feet out of the boots. All the money had been running straight out and into the room, which was now nearly filled with the gold. The devil didn't say a word. He let the general think he had gotten away with his trick. But that night the house in which Jonathan Moulton lived caught fire unexplainably. The general and his wife escaped in their nightshirts. Moulton didn't worry too much at that point—not knowing that the fire was the devil's doing. He felt sure he would be able to get his gold out all right, even if it had all melted into one lump. He assumed it would just fall into the basement, and he would be able to retrieve it after the fire burned out. He therefore refused all assistance from his neighbors, who had grudgingly offered to help. He didn't want them to discover his secret. But when the fire was all over and the whole house was burned to the ground, he could not find gold anywhere. It hadn't just melted, it had disintegrated into nothingness.

Even so, there must have been some money left somewhere, because Jonathan Moulton had enough left to build himself a new house—a lovely home with his name on it still exists in Hampton. Well known in the community as "the haunted house," it has a history of spooks and specters and sounds of various frightening kinds—everything from General Jonathan Moulton's cane taps and footsteps to his first wife's swishing skirts.

If Abigail Moulton has continued to swish through her house, she had good reason. She died under "very suspicious circumstances," and the general married again almost immediately. Not only that but he married a woman who had been his first wife's companion. Tradition has it that she was young and beautiful; but that is another of those careless statements about the general. Abigail could not have been more than fifty when she died; and Sarah, Moulton's second wife, was thirty-six when he married her, according to Joseph Dow's *History of the Town of Hampton, New Hampshire.* That is hardly what could be referred to as a glamorous young bride, especially in an era when a girl was considered to be an old maid at twenty.

The general shocked the whole countryside on the day of Abigail's funeral by stripping the dead woman of her jewels and rings, her wedding ring included. He then proceeded to give them all to Sarah when he married her. Naturally, Abigail from her grave resented it; and, naturally, she did something about it. She couldn't have been married to Jonathan Moulton for some twenty-five years without learning to be pretty cranky herself.

In the middle of the night, Sarah awoke with a start. Something—something white and spectral—was gripping her hand. She shrieked, the general came running, but not in time to keep the wraith from tearing the rings from Sarah's fingers. This incident was so well known in John Greenleaf Whittier's day that he wrote a poem about it. Entitled "The New Wife and the Old," it describes Sarah's agony thus:

> God have mercy! ice cold
> Spectral hands her own enfold,
> Drawing silently from them
> Love's fair gift of gold and gem.

Well, the general was not about to put up with any nonsense like that. He rushed about lighting candles and searching the house. He even looked outside, in case Sarah's fright (or guilty conscience) had made her confuse an otherworldly robber with a real one. But the fact that the house was still closed up tight, and that he found no footprints anywhere outside, tended to argue against this. So eventually the search was given up. The ghostly visitant had claimed her own possessions and carried them off with her, no doubt to gloat over on lonely etheric nights.

When the time came for the general to die, in 1787, the legends about him had already gained so much momentum that no one was satisfied after his burial until his grave was opened up again to see if he was still there. And sure enough, when the lid was removed, the coffin was found to be empty. The devil had collected his bet.

Obviously, such a general nuisance as General Moulton would not be able to rest in peace. And so the story that his house was haunted grew by leaps and bounds. Sarah lived on there until her death and then the place was sold to a man who moved from Portsmouth with all his servants. But he could not keep household help more than a few days, because everyone saw so many ghosts there.

Many years later, in 1919, the highway that went by the General Jonathan Moulton House had become so noisy that the occupants had the house picked up bodily and moved. It is now in a spot across the road, back in a grove of trees where it is much more private. The house had been remodeled by then and was in the beautiful condition in which it is now maintained. The gracious elderly lady who presently owns it and lives there with a friend told me that she has absolutely no trouble with haunts of any kind. Nothing around there ever goes bump in the night. This is because the ghost has been exorcized. She assured me, on the strength of a letter that was written by a descendant of the general named Augustus Moulton of Portland, that sometime during the middle of the last century Parson Milton from Newbury performed this ceremony successfully.

The devil was probably bored fooling around with Jonathan Moulton by then, anyway.

CHAPTER ELEVEN

GHOSTS IN
THE WHITE HOUSE

ABRAHAM LINCOLN IS THE MOST POPULAR GHOST in the White House; but many others have also been reported. Abigail, wife of John Adams, the second president of the United States, for instance, is a habitué. She used to be seen occasionally during the Taft Administration, passing through locked doors. And she is said to have appeared to others since. She is a very busy entity, who seems to feel it necessary, and suitable, to do her laundry in the East Room.

George Washington, of course, had nothing to do with the White House, which was not built until after his tenure of office. But George, himself, had such an interesting psychic experience that it would seem pertinent to touch on it here. The beautiful woman who appeared to him at Valley Forge may have been a ghost, or she may have been an angel, but her message was so reassuring to the great general that it may have had a lot to do with his winning the battle—and the country. Although the story of Washington's ghostly vision may be apocryphal, his close friend Anthony Sherman of Philadelphia always told it as fact. Because some of the predictions, which were published in the last century, have come true since then, it is worthy of our attention.

The experience occurred during the agonizing winter of 1777, when Washington, after several reverses, was with his troops at Valley Forge. Sherman told the story to several people and it was published in at least two newspapers. A Mormon periodical carried the account in 1856 and the *National Tribune* carried it in 1880. In the latter account, Sherman is quoted as having said that at Valley Forge, "I often saw the tears coursing down the dear commander's careworn cheeks, as he would be conversing,

with confidential officers about the condition of his poor soldiers."
There is no doubt but that Washington had much to worry him.
"No pay, no clothes, no provisions, no rum!" was the constant
and familiar complaint of all the soldiers. Washington often used
to pray in secret for aid and comfort for his hungry men, according
to Anthony Sherman.

One day he stayed in his quarters alone for hours. When he
came out, he told Sherman and another officer who was there of
the strange vision he'd just had. "I do not know whether it is
owing to the anxiety of my mind or what," he said, "but this
afternoon, as I was sitting at the table engaged in preparing a
dispatch, something seemed to disturb me. Looking up I beheld
standing opposite me a singularly beautiful female figure. So as-
tonished was I that it was some moments before I found language
to inquire the purpose of her presence."

Washington went on: "Gradually the surrounding atmosphere
seemed filled with sensations and grew luminous. Everything about me
seemed to rarify; the mysterious visitor herself became more airy
and yet more distinct to my sight than ever."

Presently the general heard a voice saying, "Son of the Republic,
look and learn!" A heavy white vapor seemed to rise, and as it
dissipated he looked upon a strange scene. Before him lay spread
out all the countries of the world, and there were billowing waves
between Europe and America. "Then," he said, "I beheld a dark
shadowy being, like an angel, standing, or rather, floating, in mid-
air between Europe and America. Dipping water out of the ocean
in the hollow of each hand, he sprinkled some upon America with
his right hand, while with his left hand he cast some on Europe.
Immediately a cloud arose from those countries, and joined in
mid-ocean. For a while it remained stationary, and then it moved
slowly westward, until it enveloped America in its murky folds.

"Sharp flashes of lightning gleamed through it at intervals; and
I heard the smothered groans and cries of the American people.
A second time the angel dipped water from the ocean and sprinkled
it out as before. The dark cloud was then drawn back to the
ocean, in whose heaving billows it sank from view. Again I heard
the mysterious voice say, 'Son of the Republic, look and learn.'
I cast my eyes upon America and beheld villages and towns and
cities springing up, one after another, until the whole land, from
the Atlantic to the Pacific, was dotted with them. Another time I

heard the mysterious voice say: 'Son of the Republic, the end of the century cometh, look and learn.'

"And with this the dark shadowy figure turned its face southward, and from Africa I saw an ill-omened specter approaching our land. It flitted slowly over every town and city. The inhabitants presently set themselves in battle array against each other. As I continued looking I saw a bright angel, on whose brow rested a crown of light on which was traced the word UNION, place an American flag between the divided nation, and say, 'Remember, ye are brethren.' Instantly, the inhabitants, casting from them their weapons, became friends once more, and united around the National Standard."

George Washington went on: "Then once more I beheld the villages, towns, and cities spring up where I had seen them before; while the bright angel planted the azure standard he had brought in the midst of them, and cried with a loud voice, 'While the stars remain and the heavens send down dew upon the earth, so long shall the Union last.' And taking from his brow the crown on which was blazoned the word UNION he placed it upon the standard, while people, kneeling down, said, 'Amen.'"

These portions of Washington's vision probably referred to the African origin of the Negro slaves, the division of sentiment among the people over the question of slavery, the Civil War, and the ultimate reunion under one flag. All this had come to pass before the date on which Sherman's story was published in the *National Tribune*. But Washington's account had gone on, and now it involved predictions which no one in 1880 even so much as suspected would ever be fulfilled:

"But I received yet another vision and another prophecy. I saw rolling and tossing between Europe and America the billows of the Atlantic, and between Asia and America lay the Pacific . . . The dark angel put a trumpet to his mouth and blew three distinct blasts, and taking water from the ocean sprinkled it upon Europe, Asia and Africa . . . Then my eyes looked upon a fearful scene. Clouds from these countries blended into one and soon enveloped America . . . Through the clouds gleamed a bright red light . . . I saw hordes of armed men marching by land and sailing by sea . . . Dimly I saw vast armies devastate whole countries, pillaging and burning great cities . . . I heard the thundering of cannon, the clashing of swords, and the shouts and cries of millions in mortal combat. . . .

"Suddenly I saw the angel upon whose forehead still shone the word UNION, and who bore our national flag in one hand and a sword in the other. She descended from Heaven attended by legions of bright spirits. Again amid the fearful noise of the conflict, I heard a voice saying, 'Son of the Republic, look and learn!' As the voice ceased the shadowy angel appeared and, for the last time, sprinkled water from the ocean on all the countries of the world.

"The angel said, 'Son of the Republic, what you have just seen is thus interpreted: Three great perils will come upon the Republic. The most fearful for her is the third; but the whole world united shall not prevail against her. Let every child of the Republic learn to live for his God, his land, and his Union.'

"With those words," concluded Washington, "the vision vanished. I started from my seat, and felt that I had seen a vision wherein had been shown to me the birth, progress, and destiny of the United States."

Anthony Sherman was so impressed with this incident that he wrote down every word of it with painstaking care right away, and he related the incident many times during his long life.

From soaring to the heights with the Father of Our Country, we now return to the White House itself. There we are back with those mundane phantoms with no great mission, who only want to continue to participate in the experience of living in a place as exciting and interesting as the home of the President of the United States.

Dolley Madison is one of these. Her most emphatic appearance is recorded as having occurred when the second Mrs. Woodrow Wilson ordered the White House gardeners to move Dolley's rose garden. In all her early nineteenth-century fashions and furbelows, President Madison's wife flounced up to the gardeners and gave them a thorough tongue lashing. They then and there desisted, and the rose garden remains exactly where it always was.

A boy ghost whose materialization was sworn to by members of President Grant's household was identified as Lincoln's son Willie, who died in the White House. His appearance came as no surprise, because several members of Grant's family believed that spirits of the dead were able to communicate with the living.

An interesting event, occurring after President Grant's death, comes from his sister, Mrs. Mary Grant Cramer. She reported that the death of Grant's widow had been foretold to her in a dream. Mrs. Cramer was living at the time with her sister, Mrs. Virginia Grant Corbin, in East Orange, New Jersey. At breakfast one morning she related an exceedingly vivid dream. She said, "Last night I thought that Mrs. Grant came to my bedside and, placing her hand on my shoulder, said impressively: 'Mary, I have come to talk with you and to say goodbye, because I am not going to be with you much longer.'"

To Mrs. Cramer's astonishment, after she had told the dream, a house guest, Mrs. Katherine Lawrence, said that she, too, had had a singular dream that same night. She thought that she, Mrs. Cramer, and Mrs. Corbin were standing together at the portal of Grant's tomb on Riverside Drive, New York City, and that there was a large crowd outside awaiting the arrival of a cavalcade of some kind. When Mrs. Grant died eight days later, the New York Sun and other papers carried the stories of these prophetic dreams.

President Garfield is said to have believed that he saw and conversed with his father after his death. As for modern witnesses to the White House phenomena, we have several employees who have admitted publicly their experiences. Lillian Rogers Parks published a book in 1961 called My Thirty Years Backstairs in the White House, and in it she testified to her belief in the truth of many of the rumors coming from the servants' quarters. She says that many who lived in the White House, as well as several of their guests, have witnessed strange goings-on.

Mrs. Parks, who is a seamstress, recalls that when she was working at the bed in the Rose Room, getting the spread ready for Britain's Queen Elizabeth II, she had an experience that sent her flying out of there with shivers. "The spread was a little too long," she writes, "and I was hemming it as it lay on the bed. I had finished one side, and was ready to start on the other, when suddenly I felt that someone was looking at me, and my scalp tightened."

She could feel something coldish behind her, but she did not have the courage to turn and look. She merely rushed out of the room in a hurry, and "didn't finish that spread until three years later."

The seamstress was not the only one among the servants who felt squeamish in that room. Katurah Brooks, who used to work on the second floor, was doing her chores there when she heard laughter coming from the bed. "It was loud laughter," Mrs. Parks writes, "and had a hollow sound, and it couldn't have come from any other place, because she was the only person in the room."

The Rose Room is always reserved for guests of highest rank, and the bed there is the one which was used by Andrew Jackson when he was President.

It would be comforting to think that such a great man as Abraham Lincoln might still be living in the White House, continuing to help guide the Ship of State. That is no doubt the main reason that so many individuals claim to have seen him or felt his presence one way or another. Yet again, perhaps he really *is* there.

Queen Wilhelmina of the Netherlands is said to have opened her door one night to a strange knock and to have seen the ghost of Lincoln standing there. Mrs. Parks says that the next morning Queen Wilhelmina told this to Franklin D. Roosevelt. He said he was not surprised, because his wife had also experienced something strange.

Mrs. Roosevelt has been reported by several people to have seen or felt Lincoln's presence. She said that when she was working at her desk in the room that had been his bedroom, she would often be aware of him standing behind her. Even when she turned around and could not see him, she still knew that he was there.

At a certain window in the Oval Room, where Lincoln stood looking out toward Virginia, deeply concerned about the Civil War, his ghost has appeared on several occasions to White House employees. Mrs. Coolidge is said to have seen him there also.

President Harry S. Truman had his quota of unaccountable experiences but he had a more prosaic explanation for them. During a television interview, his daughter Margaret once asked him: "Remember the night you heard a knock on your bedroom door in the White House?"

"Yes," said Truman, "I heard the knock and answered it about three o'clock in the morning. There wasn't anybody there. I think it must have been Lincoln's ghost walking the hall." The experience was repeated several times, he said. But, when asked about this later, Truman insisted he had been joking about the ghost, although not about the knocks. He declared that he heard many unusual knockings and other sounds before the house was reconstructed during his term of office; but he said they had all ceased after the repairs on the house were made.

President Herbert Hoover was less specific about the strange sounds he heard during his stay in the presidential mansion. He merely said that "many of them were fantastic." Theodore Roosevelt attributed his unusual experiences there to Lincoln, definitely. He said he often felt Lincoln's presence. A girl secretary who worked there in the early days of the New Deal insisted that once, in mid-afternoon, she had seen Abraham Lincoln sitting on the bed he had slept in during his lifetime. "He was pulling on his boots," she said.

Adlai Stevenson spent at least one night in Lincoln's bedroom and slept in his bed. He heard no eerie sounds and saw no apparitions. But, with typical Stevenson humor, he said the next morning that he had not slept very soundly, after picking up a book on the bedside table entitled *The Corpse Was Cold.*

There is the Lincoln ghost train tradition, which must be mentioned, even though it has never yet pulled into the White House grounds on one of its peregrinations. Actually, it is not one ghost train, but two, which are supposed to travel on various tracks of the country on a certain unhappy day in April. Both engines are old-timers with wide smokestacks and a great deal of polished brass. The entire lengths of both trains are draped with crepe, giving the impression of great shrouds on wheels. The first train carries a large band soundlessly playing its lugubrious funeral music. The second train, which follows directly on the heels (or wheels) of the first, has only a single flatcar, on which is a lonely coffin. The train is supposed to be taking the Great Emancipator to a rest he apparently has never achieved.

It is well known that Lincoln himself was undoubtedly psychic. *The Encyclopaedia Britannica* says of him, "He was occasionally subject to hours of deep silence and introspection that approached a condition of trance." His dream of his own death has been told thousands of times. He thought he heard great crying and moaning and on going to see what it was found a coffin lying in state, and inside the coffin he saw himself. This occurred just a short time before his assassination.

Under the date of April 23, 1863, the *Chicago Tribune* ran an item telling about a spiritual soiree Abraham Lincoln held in the Crimson Room at the White House for the purpose of testing the alleged supernatural powers of medium Charles E. Shockle. For about half an hour various phenomena were seen, raps were heard, tables moved. The picture of Henry Clay that hung on the wall was swayed more than a foot, and two candelabra, which had been presented to President Adams by the Bey of Algiers with no such intent in mind, were twice raised near to the ceiling.

It is typical of Lincoln's broad-mindedness that when his interest was aroused by phenomena that could not be explained in any normal way, he went ahead with his investigation, even though it was an unpopular subject. On another occasion a physical medium named Mrs. Miller was asked to visit the White House, and when she placed her hand on the big grand piano it rose into the air. As this astonishing performance continued, President Lincoln said, with his gentle smile, "I think we can hold this instrument down." Thereupon he, the Honorable D. E. Somes, a former Congressman from Maine, and an unnamed gentleman climbed up on the piano and sat down on it side by side. As soon as they were seated, Mrs. Miller again placed the palms of her hands on the piano. Instantly, even with all their added weight, the piano started to move up and down in perfect timing to Mrs. Miller's gestures. When this amazing performance was over, President Lincoln suggested that if anyone who heard of this should doubt, they "should bring such a person here and when the piano seems to rise, have him slip his foot under the leg and be convinced by the weight of the evidence resting upon his understanding."

Mrs. Miller had apparently come to the White House with Miss Nettie Coburn, who was a mental medium frequently consulted by the President during the worst crises of the war. Through her mouth when she was in trance great leaders in the spirit world purported to speak, and the advice they gave was so wise that Lincoln took it under very careful advisement. He is reported to have told Miss Coburn, "My child, you possess a most singular gift; that it is of God, I have no doubt."

To bring this account up to the present epoch, little Fala, President Franklin Roosevelt's beloved Scottie dog, is said by Lillian Rogers

Parks to have acted most queerly at his master's funeral service and to have let out "such a strange crying noise."

Naturally, White House ghost buffs are waiting to learn if there are any reports about John Fitzgerald Kennedy. So far, not even a single unaccountable rock of his famous chair has been reported.

CHAPTER TWELVE

THE JUMPING
JUMEL MANSION

HAVING SPOKEN SO RESPECTFULLY about the first President of the United States in the last chapter, I am now going to be rude enough to suggest that he was a man with emotions like any other. Rumor has it that Washington had an illegitimate daughter. She, herself, who was to become Mme. Jumel and live in one of New York's most beautiful homes, did nothing to quiet the report—in fact, she even encouraged it. Later gossip she could not have liked as much, however; for she is reputed to have hastened her husband's death so that she could marry Aaron Burr—and she is said now to haunt her old home. From such suggestions as these one might draw the conclusion that Mme. Jumel was quite a character—and she was.

The great mansion in which she lived is also rumor-ridden, as well as ghost-ridden. The famous Morris-Jumel house, presiding as it has since Revolutionary days on the highest elevation of Manhattan Island, had a colorful history before Mme. Jumel ever set foot in it. And, oddly enough, George Washington was involved with it then, too.

As recently as January 8, 1964, the ghost was seen at the old mansion, which is now preserved for the public as a museum run by the Daughters of the American Revolution. Shortly before 11:00 A.M., a group of fourteen or fifteen students from nearby P.S. 164, a predominantly Negro school at Edgecombe Avenue and 164th Street in Washington Heights, arrived for a tour of the museum. They were accompanied by their teacher, Mrs. Betty Fitzgerald.

Since the house would not be opened to the public before eleven o'clock the children wandered around the spacious lawns and box-

(Above) *An old cemetery in Machiasport, Maine. Did the late Mrs. Nelly Butler arise from here to assist her bereaved husband to find a second wife?* (Left) *The interesting antique doors of the Robert E. Lee mansion in Alexandria, Virginia. They open onto the terrace where the little ghost dog is frequently seen.*

The house in Kennebunkport,
Maine, where "Nellie," the shade
of a Quaker maid, peers
through the attic windows.

A view of the hip-roofed Bishop
Huntington house in
Hadley, Massachusetts.

The Lee Payson Smith house in Wiscasset, Maine. An elderly lady in nineteenth-century dress sometimes looks out the window shown at left.

(Above) *The General Jonathan Moulton home in Hampton, New Hampshire. Was it in this house that General Moulton's second wife awoke one night to discover something white and spectral tearing the rings from her fingers? The incident inspired John Greenleaf Whittier's poem "The New Wife and the Old."*

(Left) *Ghosts now walk in the kitchen wing of the Guibourd house, St. Genevieve, Missouri. This area of the home once served as slaves' quarters.*

The Ocean Born Mary house in Henniker, New Hampshire. Captain Pedro, a pirate of old, is buried beneath the hearthstone of the kitchen fireplace (right).

(Right) *Ghost Hannah's tombstone in the kitchen of "The Old Straw Place," Newfield, Maine. (Below) Lindenwald near Kinderhook, New York, where Aaron Burr is sometimes seen and heard in the quiet of the night.*

The Gardette-LePrêtre house in New Orleans where the Oriental splendor of a Turkish harem was captured forever in Louisiana time by a tragic mass slaying. (Photo by Chas. L. Franck)

New York City's famous Morris-Jumel mansion which dates back to pre-Revolutionary days. Old Mme. Jumel has recently been seen on the front balcony.

The author with Julio Vasquez shortly after a poltergeist began making a shambles of the warehouse in Miami, Florida, where Vasquez worked as a shipping clerk. (Miami Herald photo)

wood gardens and played on the cannon in the yard. A few girls stood on the front porch talking while waiting for someone to arrive to open the door. It was a nice day, but it began to get cold and the children were eager to go inside.

Within a short time the curator, Mrs. Emma Bingay Campbell, arrived. "When I went over to the children," she said, "to explain that they must wait for the second gardener, John Duffy, to unlock the doors, one of the girls asked, 'Why couldn't that old woman have let us in?'"

"Who?" asked Mrs. Campbell.

"That old woman who came out on the balcony."

"Yes," chimed in another girl, "that fussy old woman who told us to shut up."

"You must be mistaken," Mrs. Campbell said. "The house is empty."

She got a chorus of arguments. Four of the girls insisted that they had definitely seen a woman step out on the balcony above where they had been standing. She had told them to "shut up," in those very words.

To prove to them that the house was empty, Mrs. Campbell took the group around to the side door by which she always entered, and then she conducted them through the house. Not another soul was inside. It wasn't until they reached the upstairs hall and observed that the door onto the balcony was still padlocked and bolted that Mrs. Campbell was actually believed. Then the girls began to seek madly for another explanation of what they knew they had seen with their own eyes. What other explanation was there than that they had seen a ghost?

Mrs. Campbell and Mrs. Fitzgerald began checking with each girl as to exactly what she had observed. The stories all coincided. They had seen a woman with gray hair, dressed in a long skirt with something red at the waist, like a belt or sash. She had stepped onto the balcony and said, "Shut up!" and then, according to one girl, she had seemed to glide back inside. As to whether or not the door had been open back of her, no one had an opinion. They had all been so angry at being fussed at by the cranky stranger that most details had escaped them.

The question as to whose ghost it was did not rouble Mrs. Campbell. Obviously it was Mme. Jumel's ghost. That rich old lady who had hung onto life until the age of ninety-three, that unpleasant creature who was reputed to have allowed her husband to die of wounds so that she could marry former Vice-President of the United States Aaron Burr, that insecure, unhappy soul who had never found peace during life—isn't she the ideal entity upon whom to blame any ghostly manifestations that have been reported in the house? Mrs. Campbell thinks so.

The school children are not the only ones who have encountered her. A guard discovered her at the door to her bedroom one day; and many visitors have heard her footsteps. No other specific ghosts have been distinguished there, but with the various and numerous inhabitants over the years, there may have been some. No house in America has had a more colorful history nor been lived in or visited by a greater array of famous people. "Within its walls," says the brochure by John Kent Tilton that is handed to visitors at the museum, "has been enacted a pageant of American history."

The house is in a locality which was originally called "Harlem Heights" by the Dutch in the days of New Amsterdam and was changed to "Mount Morris" during the English ownership, before receiving the present name of Washington Heights after the Revolution. The plot of land upon which the house is situated was originally deeded in 1700 to a Dutch farmer named Jan Kiersen. The larger portion of this land was inherited at his death by his daughter Janetje, the wife of Jacob Dyckman. They sold the property in 1763 to James Carroll, who, two years later, advertised it for sale as follows: "A pleasant situated farm on the road leading to King's Bridge in the township of Harlem, York Island, containing about 100 acres; about 30 of which is woodland, a fine piece of the finest Prospect in the whole country. The land runs from River to River, there is Fishing, Oystering and Clamming at either end. There is a good house, a fine barn 33 feet long and 42 feet wide or thereabouts, an Orchard of good fruit with plenty of Quince trees that bear extraordinarily well, three good gardens the produce of which are sent to York Markets daily, as it suits. An indisputable Title will be given to the purchaser. Inquire of James Carroll, living on the Premises."

Evidently this advertisement attracted the attention of wealthy young Lieutenant Colonel Roger Morris, who purchased the estate in 1765, as a country residence for himself and his wife. She was the former Mary Philipse, rich and socially prominent, who was said at one time to have been courted by George Washington.

(Chronologically, this is the first mention of his connection with the house.) Morris erected the imposing mansion in 1765 and named it "Mount Morris." It commanded the finest view of any estate in Manhattan; one could see from the spacious grounds the East River, the Hudson and the Harlem rivers, the Palisades, Long Island, and the far distant hills of Staten Island. Of course, this house was "way out in the country" in those days when New York City occupied only the tiniest tip of the island.

In this paradise the Morrises and their four children spent their summers until the outbreak of the Revolution. Both the Morris and Philipse families were Tories, and they realized that victory for the "Rebels" meant the dissolution of their vast estates. Colonel Morris fled to England, but returned to New York in the latter part of 1777. At the instance of the British government, he was given the post of Inspector of the Claims of Refugees, which he retained until the treaty of peace was signed in 1783. Then the entire Morris family sailed to England, where they settled permanently.

As early in the war as August 1776, Mount Morris was taken over by the American troops, and General Heath and his staff were quartered there. After the disastrous Battle of Long Island, General Washington made the house his center of operations. The large octagonal drawing room at the rear of the hall was used as Washington's Military Headquarters, and four courts-martial were held there. During this time was fought the Battle of Harlem Heights in which the Continental Army won its first victory. After Washington decided to abandon the location, the British moved in and the Morris Mansion housed Sir Henry Clinton and his officers, and, at intervals, the Hessians, during the seven years the British occupied New York. When peace was restored the house and land were confiscated and sold by the Commission of Forfeiture.

During the following quarter of a century the house was sold and resold several times. Renamed Calumet Hall for a time, it served as a tavern that was a stopping place for the stagecoaches en route to Albany. It was the home of an unknown farmer when President Washington paid a visit to his old headquarters and entertained his cabinet members, John Adams, Alexander Hamilton, Henry Knox, and their wives, among others, at dinner.

Alexander Hamilton was later on to figure in some of the rumors about Mme. Jumel, for she was said to be closely associated

with him for a while and, gossip suggested, "overly-intimate." Mme.
Jumel herself may have encouraged, or even started, some of the
many stories about her that existed during her lifetime. It has been
claimed that she was born at sea of mysterious and unknown
parentage, that she was the daughter of Napoleon Bonaparte, that
she was of royal blood. And we mustn't forget her own favorite
story—about the father of her country. Oddly enough, the latter
is the only rumor which would have any possible foundation in
fact, for pictures of her in her maturity look so much like George
Washington that it is uncanny.

She probably preferred even the most fantastic false reports about
her birth to the truth—for she was undoubtedly the illegitimate
daughter of somebody. Her mother, Phoebe Kelley, was a girl of
the streets in Providence, Rhode Island; and John Bowen, the
sailor with whom she lived when he was in town, was away at sea
much of the time. Yet Phoebe's offspring, the first of which she
bore at the age of fourteen, continued to arrive with a certain
regularity.

Betsy Bowen, who was to become Mme. Jumel, was born in
1775, when her mother was eighteen. Because Phoebe kept such a
disorderly home, Betsy was sent to a workhouse. She grew up to
be the handsomest girl in Providence, with an all-consuming desire
to get out of the poverty and disrepute which had characterized
her early years. Still, her ambitions for better things did not stop
her from having an illegitimate child before she ever left her home
town. She named him George Washington Bowen. Was this because
of patriotism, or because she had been told by her mother that her
father was the famous figure and she wished to give public notice
to that effect? Whatever her reason, she soon abandoned her child
and went to New York. There her beauty and dash gained her
the money and grandeur of which she had dreamed. Unfortunately,
she never achieved the thing she wanted most in life—social acceptance.

In New York Betsy Bowen first became the mistress, or perhaps
the wife, of a Captain de la Croix. He took her to France, where
she soon adopted fetching French ways and learned to wear modish
clothes. Growing tired of de la Croix, she left him and returned to
New York; and it was then that she assumed the name Eliza
Brown. Along with her old name, she shed all contact with her

low-born relatives—for a time. She was to need them for companionship in later years.

Stephen Jumel also was a storybook character in his youth. A Frenchman who had at one time owned a large plantation in Santo Domingo, he had been obliged to flee because of an insurrection there. Arriving in the United States a comparatively poor man, he soon amassed a new fortune as a wine merchant. In 1800, when he met Eliza Brown, he was about forty-five years old, a graceful giant of a man, conspicuous, boisterous, and one of the richest businessmen in New York. And he was a bachelor.

Eliza became his mistress, and for four years he flaunted her in the face of local society. He even provided a large yellow coach, with four white horses and postilions in livery, in which she used to ride, dressed in outrageous finery. However, even by denying her shoddy past, refusing to recognize any of her numerous relatives, and acquiring a rich lover, she still could not gain respectability. So she determined to marry Jumel, sure that the sanctity of marriage with such a wealthy man would bring her the acceptance she so ardently desired.

One day Eliza suddenly showed evidence of great pain. "Oh, my God," she screamed, "get the doctor quick."

Jumel rushed for a physician, who prescribed various medications, but nothing seemed to help her. By the following day, she appeared to be in constant agony. Her forehead wet with sweat, she gasped and struggled; then finally she lay back inert on her bed. For another whole day she was in a stupor, barely moving, hardly seeming to breathe. Jumel was frantic as he sat beside the bed and held her hand, or ran here and there trying to find something that would help her. Finally she made an effort to speak. He held his ear close to her mouth as she whispered with great effort, "I know I am dying. Please give me my last request."

"Anything, darling, anything," Stephen answered, tears in his eyes.

"Please let me die as Mrs. Stephen Jumel. Please marry me." She barely got the words out, and then fell limp and almost lifeless.

The service was performed as quickly as arrangements could be made, and a tiny smile crept to the lips of the dying woman as she gazed lovingly at her wedding ring.

When Jumel returned after seeing the priest to the door, Eliza was sitting up in her bed with a mirror in her hand, primping and arranging her bedraggled hair. "Thank you, dear husband," she said with a wicked, and perfectly healthy grin. "You've given me what I've always wanted from you." And she polished the ring on her shoulder with a flourish.

Jumel was a Roman Catholic, and, anyway, he loved the girl. So he allowed his "marriage Italian style" to remain in effect. But although she was now Mrs. Jumel, Eliza was not accepted by New York society. People who had never approved of her as a mistress certainly could not now tolerate her as a wife. Perhaps, she decided in desperation, if she had an elaborate house in which to entertain she would be invited to the homes of the snobs. And so she encouraged her husband to look around for a suitable estate where they could live in luxury. They discovered the Robert Morris house and bought it in 1810; then they had it rebuilt, refitted, and lavishly furnished as a country home of elegance.

But an estate didn't help. People did not accept or return their invitations. Eliza and Stephen Jumel rattled around in the big old house, which only impressed their isolation on them more than ever. Mme. Jumel's solution, which was really not a solution at all, was to begin a custom that continued for the rest of her life: she asked her poor relations to send their children to keep her company. First, she took her stepsister's daughter, Mary Bowen, renaming her Mary Eliza, to raise as a daughter.

After five years of isolation and neglect in the great mansion, the Jumels, accompanied by Mary Eliza, left for Paris. This could have been a wonderful move on their part, for the French nobility welcomed them with open arms. Unfortunately, Eliza allowed herself to become too ardent a Bonapartist at a time when Napoleon was in exile. She displayed her sympathy for the cause of his return too openly, and apparently she was banished by the king for this reason. Whatever the cause, she suddenly returned to New York after a year in France, to live in the isolation of the Morris-Jumel mansion again. And this she certainly would not have done by choice. There is another theory—that she and her husband had a great fight, and he sent her home while he remained in Paris. This doesn't sound like them at all. Eliza was the ruling force in that family, and she would more likely have banished *him* if there had been a quarrel. Besides, Stephen apparently worked to get her reinstated into the good graces of the king, for eventually she was allowed to return to France. This time she remained for five brilliant years.

No one knows why Madame came home after that, but she did, although Stephen stayed in Paris some years longer. He gave her his power of attorney, and she became a businesswoman, eventually acquiring in her name everything that he owned. He was nominally a pauper after that, but he never knew it, for she handled all the business, and she did it very well. She actually managed to run up the value of his real estate holdings from one million to three million dollars in three years.

Her efforts to assuage her loneliness were less successful. As William Henry Shelton says in *The Jumel Mansion,* "She needed someone to live with, to be social with, to quarrel with, to drink with. The solitary life of this woman, of ample wealth, in her great house, after her first return from France, is almost unbelievable at this time. The neighbor families held aloof from her and she knew that their doors were closed to her. The efforts she made to secure companionship in the house were pathetic." Eventually she married off Mary Eliza to Nelson Chase (who was, many years later, to figure so prominently in a suit with George Washington Bowen for Mme. Jumel's money); and she planned that the Chases would come to live with her. She also took in other nieces and raised them. Shelton says: "At each of the marriages of her nieces, she stipulated that the young people were to come and live with her at the mansion. In each case she guaranteed an income, and she had definite ideas of what the income of young married people should be . . . but such incomes were never paid. She gathered each pair under her roof, and supported them lavishly, quite regardless of cost, but she held the purse-strings and kept them like children dependent upon her. The husbands were encouraged to live in idleness. There was no need of work for them. There was an abundance of everything at the mansion."

And so went the years. Stephen Jumel eventually returned home to live, an old man now. He and his wife occasionally managed to meet a few people of prominence, such as Aaron Burr, some years after his term in Washington. But they had no friends.

About the middle of May 1832, Stephen, playing the country gentleman and supervising the work on his estate, was riding on top of a load of hay, when he lost his balance and fell off the cart. He was so seriously injured that he died a few days later, on May

22. The fact that he had been subjected to the then universal practice of "bleeding" to reduce his fever probably hastened his end. At least, that is the charitable way to tell the story. Gossip has it that Madame encouraged her husband's death by tearing the bandages from his body and allowing him to bleed to death. William Cary Duncan, author of the book *The Amazing Madame Jumel,* is very indignant about this calumny. He thinks there "is not an atom of evidence to support any such suspicion. . . ." But the story persists.

After the funeral Eliza was either lonely or restless or both. She had with her one young relative, Mary Marilla, but that was not company enough for her. So, she sent for the Chases. Duncan says that, "Despite her increased household, the widow was still uneasy and far from happy. People said there was a ghost in the house— the ghost of the 'murdered' Stephen—and that the specter would allow Madame no peace so long as she remained there." So, as if to substantiate this eerie tale, she closed the mansion early in the fall of 1832 and took an apartment for herself and the Chases in New York City. With this move she seems suddenly to have tossed off her widow's weeds. Aaron Burr, who was then a poor, lonely little old man of seventy-eight, and a social outcast like Mme. Jumel, appeared on the scene again, and she determined to marry him. Her ambition could now aspire to such heights as a former Vice President of the United States; but I don't think there is any evidence that she made this decision before her husband's death.

She did not have to trick Burr to get him. After all, she was now a wealthy woman. She did have to settle a lot of money on him, however. The wedding was solemnized in the small parlor, or tea room, of the Morris-Jumel mansion in 1833, when the bride was fifty-eight years old. Despite Burr's advanced age—and he was twenty years his wife's senior—when Eliza decided to divorce him after a marriage of short duration, she charged him with "various matrimonial offences at divers times with divers females." The divorce was granted just a few days before Burr died.

Mme. Jumel lived on until 1865, when she was ninety-three years of age. Her eccentricities had degenerated into genuine insanity by then, and she was kept in seclusion during her later years. Madame had always been particularly vain, and Shelton speaks of "The vanity that demanded that her poor withered face should be powdered and rouged every day as she lay on her deathbed." Is it this overwhelming conceit that has refused to allow her to give up her ghostly hold on life? Or is she still searching for companionship? Perhaps it is just the fascination of her old home that causes her to remain in it and to haunt it.

That she did haunt it was reported as early as three years after her demise by a Mademoiselle Nitschke, who was governess for Matilde Elizabeth Georgiana Péry, a child of one of the nieces who lived in the Morris-Jumel mansion. Mlle. Nitschke wrote:

"I came to live at the mansion three years after Madame Jumel died, or about 1868. My room was at first on the third story and the schoolroom was on the same floor. Little Matilde was supposed to study for half an hour and then play for half an hour, but at any moment Mrs. Péry might snap her whip under the window and call us to drive in a rattle-trap wagon.

"At this time Nelson Chase would rise at five o'clock in the morning and make the halls ring with profanity calling for his breakfast. Nelson Chase ate at one time, the Pérys at another, and Will Chase and his family still later. The three families were not always on speaking terms. I was told not to speak to Mrs. Will Chase or her children. After a little time I was moved down to the 'Lafayette Room,' to be nearer Mrs. Péry, who was in nightly terror of the ghost of Madame Jumel, which she claimed came with terrible rappings between twelve and one o'clock or about midnight.

"Mrs. Péry would come to my room in the night in great excitement to escape the ghost. I would ask her if she did not fear to leave her daughter, but she said Matilde slept soundly and never heard it. One night she insisted on my coming to their bedroom and awaiting the ghost. I always told them there was no such thing as a ghost.

"On that particular night the trouble began as early as seven o'clock in the evening. They had just come up from supper when Mrs. Péry rushed into the hall trembling with fright and calling, 'Mademoiselle!' She had seen or heard some manifestation by which she claimed to know that the ghost was going to make a night of it.

"At about the same time, probably hearing the cries, Mr. Péry came up the stairs from the kitchen where he had been toasting cheese. He disliked to sleep in the room in question, claiming that Madame Jumel had come to the side of his bed in white. At my suggestion they sent for the gardener, who lived in one of the gatehouses, for an additional witness. With his help I expected to prove to them that their fears were groundless, and that what they thought they heard, they did not hear at all.

"It was a still night outside, a warm September night without a breath of wind; and it was also very quiet inside as the hour drew on to midnight. No one had broken the silence for some moments by a spoken word. Mr. Péry was pretending to read from a book. He was seated in the middle of the room in a light chair, with nothing about the legs to conceal anything. Suddenly there were loud raps like the sound of a mallet striking under the floor, and directly, seemingly, under Mr. Péry's chair, from which he leaped as if he had been shot.

"I had told them when the ghost came to ask if it wished to have prayers said for it, so I put the question, 'Do you want to have prayers said for you?' This was answered by three knocks, which is the knock-language for 'yes.' The raps that answered to 'yes' and 'no' seemed to be in the walls, now on one side of the room and now on the other. The manifestations, as I stated, began with heavy raps on the floor under Mr. Péry's chair, and they were followed by a clatter of what sounded like a skeleton hand drumming on the panes of the east front window. At one time during the manifestations this same drumming by the skeleton hand seemed to come from the room where Matilde slept, but the clatter seemed to be on some object of tin instead of on glass. I stepped to the door and looked in. Even as I looked, the tapping continued on the tin slop-pail and then ceased altogether. The child was sleeping soundly and Mrs. Péry thought I was very brave to enter the room at all."

And so, along with the rumors about Madame Jumel that flew when she was living are the questions that she has presented since her death. Did she actually tear the bandages off her wounded husband and leave him to bleed to death? Does she still haunt the old mansion in which she lived so unhappily for so many years? And if she does, why does she?

CHAPTER THIRTEEN

OCEAN BORN MARY

ANOTHER COLORFUL AND CONTROVERSIAL American ghost is Ocean Born Mary—a tall, red-haired, green-eyed specter spectacular enough to make sickly shades out of all the rest. The main question about her is whether or not it is she who haunts her old home in Henniker, New Hampshire. Somebody probably does—when all the evidence is in. But is it Mary?

The story of Ocean Born Mary has always been one of my favorites, and I'd hate to have to give up her ghost; but there seems to be a concerted effort going on to suppress her. I am also finding it difficult to acquire evidence that will substantiate her as a haunt.

The legend about her romantic birth seems to be intact, however, and it is a fascinating story in itself. Mary's allegedly endless existence began aboard the little sailing vessel "Wolf" in July 1720. The ship was en route from Ireland to the New World with a party of Scotch-Irish emigrants. Early on the morning of July 28, when his ship was in sight of the Massachusetts Coast with a safe journey almost completed, Captain James Wilson sighted a ship flying the Jolly Roger, that grinning skull on a black field which presaged the arrival of pirates. Soon the "Wolf" was boarded by evil Captain Pedro and his men, who threatened to make everyone aboard walk the plank.

Just at that moment a sudden whimpering was heard below deck—the cry of a newborn infant. It was the young daughter of Captain Wilson, venturing into the world several weeks before she had been expected, undoubtedly thinking it would be her only chance to see a real, live pirate. Captain Pedro, a most unusual buccaneer, grew soft and sentimental at the scene and wept exquisite tears. The birth at such a propitious moment inspiring him, he agreed to spare the ship and all on board if Mrs. Wilson would promise to name the baby "Mary," after his wife. When she said she would, he took his men and departed. The "Wolf" passengers, cheered at his leaving, were depressed when he soon climbed back on board their ship. But this time he brought valuable presents in his arms: dresses he had obviously ripped from the bodies of former victims, plumed bonnets that had once graced heads now long in the briny deep, a bracelet glittering with jewels. There was also a swatch of sumptuous greenish-blue brocade silk—for Mary's wedding dress. When appreciation for these gifts was duly shown by Captain Wilson and his wife Elizabeth, the pirate went on his way again, and this time his ship really sailed off into the mists.

This signal deliverance from pirates was commemorated as a day of thanksgiving for a generation or two in Londonderry, New Hampshire, the town in which the passengers settled. Captain Pedro never forgot his little protégée, and kept in touch with Mary as she grew to beautiful young womanhood. And she grew, and she grew, and she grew—to a full six feet in height. When she was eighteen Ocean Born Mary was married to Thomas Wallace, a man who stood hands higher than she. They had four sons, Thomas, Robert, William, and James; and perhaps a daughter called Elizabeth after Mary's mother, although her name is not in the records.

A description of Mary as she was when she lived in Henniker, New Hampshire, is given in *The History of the Town of Henniker* by Leander W. Cogswell. He writes: "She was remembered as being quite tall, resolute, and determined; of strong mind, quick of comprehension, with a strong brogue, and full of humor. She was florid of complexion, bright eyed, and elegant in her manners to the last of her life. Her younger life experience was wonderful in toils and hardships; but her last years were sunny and happy." Her sons all grew up to be, as Cogswell aptly if stalely phrases it, "pillars of the community."

How Mary's path happened to end in the town of Henniker brings us back to legend, and to Captain Pedro again. The pirate is reputed to have decided to retire—as far inland as he could go because he was a hunted man. He bought one hundred acres of land in the hilly country several miles out from Henniker, and had his ship's carpenters build him a mansion thereon.

But what was a home without a woman? Undoubtedly Captain Pedro's wife had long ago left him; pirates' spouses were notoriously fickle. And so he contacted Mary, whose husband had died, and asked her to come and live with him—and be his housekeeper. (He was probably quite an old pirate by then.) Mary came to Henniker with her four sons and there she lived until she was ninety-four. And then she died.

Legend and fact are so intertwined here that it is difficult to separate one from the other. But there is enough truth to the story of Ocean Born Mary's uncommon birth that it is taught in the schools of New Hampshire. For evidence, a piece of the silk brocade dress she was married in has been saved and is on display at her home.

The Ocean Born Mary house is covered with clapboard with a weathered finish that gives it a spectral look. That the construction was truly by ship's carpenters is indicated by the choice, hand-wrought wood paneling inside—and by the definite roll in the kitchen floor. David Russell of Chelmsford, Massachusetts, the present owner of the house, says that many captains had their houses built with floors like this, to remind them of the sloping decks of their ships. This floor actually looks as if it had warped, except that it has such a large smooth curve, and the wood is so neatly joined, that it obviously was constructed that way deliberately. Russell also points out the H-L hinges, called "Crusader's Crosses," on many of the doors. They were hex signs to keep witches away.

When Mary and her captain lived there, they could very well have wished for hex signs to remove lawless pirates. There was always the rumor, which still exists, that Captain Pedro had buried huge sums of money somewhere on his property. His old crew members were said to be constantly sneaking around trying to find it, and there was frequent violence of one kind or another around the place. After all, Pedro did not reform just because he had retired from buccaneering. He ultimately came to a most untidy, but surely well-deserved, end with a ruffian's knife in his back. His last wish was to be buried under the hearthstone in the kitchen, and that is where Mary is supposed to have put him. Perhaps all his money was buried there with him. Some people will tell you so.

"Why haven't you removed the slab to find out?" I asked Mr. Russell. His reply delighted me.

"If I own what is supposedly buried under the stone of Captain Pedro's grave," he said, "I'm a rich man now. If I dig for it and find it, the government will take most of it. If I dig and discover that there's nothing there, I have nothing. So I'll let the story stay as it is."

It is said that anyone who disturbs this hearthstone will meet death. Russell repeated what Louis ("Gus") Roy, the former owner, told him about this. A man named Tony Eddy from Gloucester, Massachusetts, came and asked Gus to let him dig up the stone and get the money—which they would share evenly. Roy had not figured the problem out the way that Russell has, so he agreed to let Eddy do the digging. The Gloucester man went home for his equipment, and then, the week before he was to return and do the work, he was killed in a strange manner. While he was lying under his car making repairs, the jack slipped and the car fell on him.

When Gus Roy came to Henniker and bought the Ocean Born Mary house he was very "antique minded," writing occasionally for magazines on the subject. He soon opened the interesting old home to the public, hoping to make a living from it. After that an occasional magazine or book would carry a mention of the ghost of the lovely Mary and how she watches over her former abode. According to Roy, there was a tradition that on Halloween every year Mary would dash up in a carriage drawn by four horses and rush over to a well and drop something into it. Since she lived right there, this does not make much sense, but what yarn spun of fictional floss ever does? Roy said he had not seen Mary himself, but that his mother often had. He told several anecdotes revealing how Mary protected her old home, noting that in the past she had frightened off a number of tenants who had shoddy furniture, or whose housekeeping was less than desirable. But she had sheltered him from the moment she learned that he had respect for the age and beauty of the house.

Once, Gus said, when he had been there but a short time, he was about to throw an old paper bag into the fire. But he suddenly felt constrained, as if a hand had grasped his arm. It refused to let go until he had examined the contents of the bag carefully. He found in it several pounds of blasting powder!

During the hurricane that hit New England in 1938, Mr. Roy saw that the small garage he had built was swaying precariously and that his car would be crushed unless he could support the building in some way. He worked fast in the drenching torrent, propping up the garage from the outside as best he could, and then he hurried back to the house. Then he learned that his mother, watching out the window, had seen a tall woman working hard beside him.

To my knowledge there had never been any other reports published about this haunting except those originating with Gus Roy and his mother. But Roy's stories were titillating enough. I was charmed by the mental picture I had of the valiant Mary still protecting her home after all those years, I accepted it as probably at least as historically true as the legend of her birth. When I went to the house I was much impressed by its dark and brooding aspect, obviously carefully cultivated by the choice of exterior finish. A perfect setting for a perfect story, I thought.

With all this romantic buildup, I stepped inside the front door and was greeted by David Russell and his wife Corinne, a typical, amiable New England couple. I told them I had come to interview Ocean Born Mary's ghost, and they immediately informed me she was not there. I have seldom been so taken aback. Then, very pleasantly but very firmly, Mr. Russell told me that Mary's ghost was not in the house, had never been there and was not likely to be there in the future. Although I could hardly accept it, I was assured that all accounts of the phantom had come from Gus Roy's fertile brain. Mrs. Russell said that she had worked for Roy before she and her husband bought the house from him; that she had taken care of him during his last illness; and that he had told her himself he had invented the ghost so that people would want to come to see the place.

Both Mr. and Mrs. Russell assured me that they feel just the opposite about the story and do not want the house to be known for anything but its beauty and its exciting history. They showed me a hole in a window caused by a rifle fired at the "haunted house" on Halloween. On that night it has become the custom for young people from Henniker and other nearby towns to come and sit on the lawn and wait for the specter to arrive in her coach. It is not uncommon for boys to throw rocks at the house, daring Mary to come out and show herself to them. The youths not only damage the property but litter it as well, so naturally they are not encouraged.

I was quite aware of the possibility that the Russells were suppressing evidence of conceivable ghostly activity because it was in their interest to do so; therefore, I went straight into the town of

Henniker to learn what I could from local residents. And there
my sentimental fancies were shattered completely. I talked to several
people who assured me there had never been a word about a ghost
until Gus Roy came.

Mrs. Robert Goss said that her family and her husband's family
for three generations had all lived in Henniker, and she had never
heard any one of them say a word about a ghost connected with
the Ocean Born Mary house. The place itself was well known, but
not its apparitions, if any. Mrs. Goss's stepmother, Anna Newton
Garland, had lived to be over a century old and had known
and often discussed almost everything about the town's history; but
she had never once spoken of Mary's ghost.

I talked to Mr. Forrest Dowlin, age seventy-six, who said that his
grandfather, James S. Dowlin, had bought the Ocean Born Mary
place in 1866. He himself had lived on the farm when he was
young, but the house had never given any evidence of being haunted.

"There was an old well in the cellar," he said, "and when I
was a boy about twelve or fourteen years old, grandfather got the
idea it was dangerous and put me to work at it. I drove the oxen
to haul stone and filled it up completely." Gus Roy, who came there
from LaCrosse, Wisconsin, bought the house from Mr. Dowlin's
family in 1917, and then, Dowlin said, "Roy had a man take
out all those stones and clean out the well, trying to find the
money." It appears that Roy and his efforts to locate buried gold
on the property were rather amusing to the townspeople.

So that's where the saga of the spurious spook stood in the
summer of 1966 when Hans Holzer's book, *Yankee Ghosts,* came
out. In it Corinne Russell is stated to have contacted Holzer in
October 1963 to tell him their house was haunted and to ask him
to come on Halloween to see if the ghost could be contacted.
Holzer quotes Mrs. Russell as telling him, when he visited them
in December 1963: "Our caretaker dropped a space heater all
the way down the stairs at the Ocean Born Mary house, and when
it reached the bottom, the kerosene and the flames started to burn
the stairs and climb the wall. There was no water in the house,
so my husband went out after snow. While I stood there looking
at the fire and powerless to do anything about it, the fire went
right out all by itself right in front of my eyes; when my husband
got back with the snow it was out. It was just as if someone
had smothered it with a blanket."

When I was there Mrs. Russell had told me this same story and I had thought, "Obviously Mary is still protecting the house." But Mrs. Russell had said nothing to imply that she had agreed with me.

In *Yankee Ghosts* it is stated that Mr. Russell had related an incident that occurred the first night he ever slept in the Lafayette room upstairs. His dog was with him. "Just as I lay down in bed," Russell said, "I heard very heavy footsteps. They sounded to me to be in the two rooms which we had just restored, on the same floor. I was quite annoyed, almost frightened, and went into the rooms, but there was nobody there or anywhere else in the house."

A few weeks after that Mr. Russell was in the same room getting undressed when he heard somebody pound on his door. "I said to myself, oh, it's only the house settling, and I got into bed. A few minutes later, the door knob turned back and forth. I jumped out of bed, opened the door, and there was absolutely nobody there."

So now, I wonder after reading this, where was I? I wrote to the Russells to ask them which account of their experiences I was to believe. Their reply came through a lawyer, stating that "Mr. and Mrs. Russell deny that there is any such ghost or other phenomenon associated with the Ocean Born Mary house. Mr. and Mrs. Russell deny the information which you have apparently received from Mr. Holzer's book and further deny that they were instrumental in having him prepare or present any of this information."

Hans Holzer, however, writes me that "every word I quoted Mrs. Russell as saying in my book is on tape, there is correspondence where they solicited my coming, etc. on the basis of there being a ghost . . . but when I last spoke to her she admitted that a lawyer representing a descendant of Mary Wallace had intimidated her and therefore she was changing her story. . . ."

So what conclusions may we draw from all this? We seem to have our choices, any of which might land us in jail. It appears that, even if we want to do so, we are not going to be allowed to maintain that Ocean Born Mary haunts her old home. Would you believe Captain Pedro?

CHAPTER FOURTEEN

THE BELL WITCH

POLTERGEIST IS A WORD which literally means "noisy ghost." Completely unexplainable activity will suddenly begin in a certain home and go on for days, weeks, or months, and then will cease as mysteriously as it began. Because no explanation has ever been found for it, the phenomenon is stuck with the odd-sounding name, although frequently there is no indication of a ghost in any way connected with it—a few dishes flying about the house, or bottle caps popping, or furniture falling over, being the extent of the activity.

In some cases, however, poltergeists have revealed that there was a conscious intelligence behind their activities, even to the point that unexplained voices have been heard speaking sensible words, rappings have answered questions by code, and other manifestations have occurred that have been too varied and too obviously thought out to have been without conscious direction of some kind. The Bell Witch is the prime example of this type of ghostly activity. For a period of four years it tortured and persecuted the John Bell family of Tennessee with unrelenting fury. Rarely seen, except in the form of a rabbit, or bird, or dog, it was heard and felt by hundreds of people, including neighbors of the haunted family and many curious visitors from other communities. Even General Andrew Jackson came to see if the unpleasant tales he had heard about the Bell Witch were true. They were.

In the early part of the last century a prosperous farmer named John Bell, who owned a thousand fine acres on the south bank of the Red River near Adams, a small town in Robertson County, Tennessee, was living the *dolce vita*. He had a loving wife, Lucy Williams Bell, and eight handsome children. The Bells were Baptists who lived good Christian lives and raised their children to be upright citizens. John had the reputation for being strictly honest, and was one of the wealthiest and most influential men in his community. Then suddenly, in the year 1817, the affliction which was to become known as the "Bell Witch" descended upon him and his family.

The first evidence occurred one beautiful day when John Bell, walking through his cornfield, was confronted by an animal unlike anything he had ever seen before. It looked somewhat like a dog, but it was not a dog. It was sitting between the corn rows, gazing steadfastly at him. Raising his gun, John fired at the creature, but it vanished. Some days later he observed a very large fowl, which he took to be a wild turkey, perched on the fence. He ran into the house for his gun, but as he came within shooting distance, the bird flapped its wings and flew away. He then saw that it was not a turkey, but an eerie bird of enormous size.

At the house the disturbances now began with knockings and scrapings on the outside of the doors and windows. Then the sound moved inside, and week after week an invisible rat seemed to be gnawing vigorously on the various bedposts, or an equally invisible dog clawed on the floor. The noise grew in volume and moved from room to room, always stopping when a search for the cause got under way. About a year after it began, the noise had so increased that it fairly shook the house. At nightfall, the coverings began to be pulled off the beds. Next, according to a diary of the case written years afterward by John's youngest son, Richard Williams Bell, the invisible power began "slapping people on the face, especially those who resisted the action of pulling the cover from the bed, and those who came as detectives to expose the trick. The blows were heard distinctly, like the open palm of a heavy hand, while the sting was keenly felt, and it did not neglect to pull my hair, and make Joel squeal as often."

Williams, as Richard Williams Bell was usually called, was only about six years old when the manifestations began. His brothers Joel and Drewry were older than he, his sister Elizabeth was twelve, and John, Jr., was twenty-four at the time. Jesse was married and so was another daughter, Esther, whose husband was Bennett Porter. These two families lived nearby. Zadok had been educated for the bar and was already practicing law. Another boy, Benjamin, had died young.

Elizabeth, commonly known as "Besty," was a chubby girl, already beginning to show evidence of the beauty she later attained. According to Williams, "She was a light-hearted, romping lass, whose roguish prettiness and mischievous glances made the hearts of the neighborhood boys go pittypat." Even her handsome bachelor teacher, Professor Richard Powell, was much impressed with her, and took every opportunity to praise her virtues to her mother, telling Mrs. Bell what a bright, sweet girl Betsy was. Powell, of course, was an "older man," but a playmate of Betsy's named Joshua Gardner was already known as a beau of hers. This young man, also described as handsome, "was graceful in appearance and cultured in manners, and very entertaining socially. He was of a good family, and had won the distinction of being the sprightliest youth in school. Everyone conceded that Josh was a fine fellow who would make his way in the world, and his attentions to Betsy were not displeasing to the old folks nor her brothers."

It is hard to believe that one who was attractive and popular could be the focal point for a poltergeist, for when they do center on a young girl she is usually a misfit with neurotic tendencies. But there is no doubt that it was Betsy about whom the witch's manifestations revolved, even to the point that she received most of the abuse. It is usual in poltergeist cases for one person, often a child in puberty, to be the focus of its activity. Parapsychologists suggest that the power or force that causes the phenomena comes from this individual. The child is often blamed for consciously producing the phenomena in a spirit of mischief, and in many instances this is undoubtedly true. There is no question but that Betsy Bell received a great deal of blame for having caused the ruckus in her home—until it was made clear in each instance that most of the manifestations were physically impossible for her to have produced.

Such events as cannot possibly be accomplished physically by the child are explained by the parapsychologist as being inspired by him subconsciously. If the young person has suppressed hatreds, or tensions, or unresolved problems, it is thought that some portion of his subconscious mind may split off and become active independently from his body, producing the manifestations. It would seem from all descriptions of Betsy that no young girl was less likely to have suppressed hatreds, or tensions, or unresolved problems, but that has not kept psychologist and psychical researcher Nandor Fodor from suspecting that her subconscious mind was responsible for the Bell Witch. Since there seemed no overt reason to blame this on Betsy, Fodor invented the possibility that perhaps her father may have inflicted some moral offense on her which rankled in her mind. Since John Bell was the recipient of the worst torture the witch could bestow—even to the point of death—Fodor believed that her father somehow must have done something to Betsy so horrible that she consciously refused to accept it, and had chastised him subconsciously in this unorthodox manner.

The far-reaching activity of the witch, who roamed the whole of Robertson County, and the fact that it operated just as violently even when Betsy was not around, makes Fodor's theory seem a bit unsophisticated. But what other explanation can be offered for the Bell Witch? Frankly, no one knows. Dr. Fodor's conclusion is that here, "Obviously, we are dealing with facts for which we have no adequate theories within normal or abnormal psychology."

In his diary, Richard Williams Bell presented many of the arguments current at that time about the cause of the phenomena. He was thirty-six when he wrote down his recollections, and those of his brothers and sisters. He called his account "Our Family Trouble," and had no plans for it ever to be published. But eventually there seemed to be so many misrepresentations rife about the Bell Witch that his heirs allowed his diary to be printed in order to clear up the misconceptions. A local editor, M. V. Ingram, the one to whom it was given for publication, had been acquainted with the story from early childhood and had often heard it related by the surviving members of John Bell's family. To corroborate the diary, he interviewed every witness or descendant of a witness—and they ran into the hundreds—that he could find. Then he published the manuscript in a small volume with a large title: *Authenticated History of the Famous Bell Witch. The Wonder of the 19th Century, and Unexplained Phenomenon of the Christian Era. The Mysterious Talking Goblin that Terrorized the West End of Robertson County, Tennessee, Tormenting John Bell to His Death. The Story of Betsy Bell, Her Lover and the Haunting Sphynx*. Clarksville, Tennessee, 1894.

Another book, *The Bell Witch, A Mysterious Spirit*, was written by Charles Bailey Bell, M.D., a prominent Tennessee physician and the grandson of John, Jr. It was published in 1934, the same year that a Federal Writers Project was undertaken on the case. This book features the many "wonderful things" prophesied by the spirit, many of which came true. These include the advent of the Civil War, emancipation of the Negroes, the rise of the United States as the leader of the world, and the two World Wars. Also predicted was the ultimate and total destruction of our civilization in a rapidly increasing heat, followed by a mighty explosion. Fortunately, this prediction is not dated, but the one regarding the Second World War proved to be dated correctly within four years.

In his diary, Williams recalls, "The strange appearances and uncommon sounds had been seen and heard by different members of the family at times, some year or two before I knew anything about it, because . . . Father, believing it was some mischievous person trying to frighten the family, never discussed the matter in the presence of the younger children, hoping to catch the prankster. Then, after the demonstrations became known to all of us, Father enjoined secrecy upon every member of the family, and it was kept a profound secret until it became intolerable."

Williams' first unpleasant personal experience with the witch occurred when he was awakened by something pulling him by the hair, raising him and giving him the feeling as if the top of his head had been taken off. "Immediately," he writes, "Joel yelled out in great fright, and next Elizabeth was screaming in her room, and after that something was continually pulling at her hair after she retired to bed."

These violent activities continued for some long time, but the family kept strict secrecy about them. Eventually they decided that they needed help. They called in James Johnson, their nearest neighbor and most intimate friend, to help solve the mystery. It was Mr. Johnson who made the discovery that the agency behind the manifestations was intelligent. He listened attentively to all the noises it made, particularly a sound like the licking of lips, and gulping, and "that which appeared like someone sucking air through the teeth" and he "adjured" it in the name of the Lord. This entreaty silenced the noise for a considerable time, then it began again with renewed vigor. After that "the persecutions of Elizabeth were increased to an extent that excited serious apprehensions." In fact, Williams writes in his quaint fashion:

"This vile, heinous, unknown devil, torturer of human flesh, that preyed upon the fears of people like a ravenous vulture, spared her not, but rather chose her as a shining mark for an exhibition of its wicked stratagem and devilish tortures. And never did it cease to practice upon her fears, insult her modesty, stick pins in her body, pinching and bruising her flesh, slapping her cheeks, dishevelling and tangling her hair, tormenting her in many ways until she surrendered that most cherished hope which animates every young heart." [More of that cherished hope later.]

Because the phenomena ceased temporarily when the invisible agent was spoken to, Johnson inferred that it understood human language. He advised John Bell to invite in other friends and form a committee of investigation. The main job of the committee was to keep a close watch on every member of the family to determine if one of them was playing pranks. But when the committee was put into operation "all of their wits were stifled, the demonstrations all the while increasing in force, and sister was so severely punished that Father and Mother became alarmed for her safety when alone, and the neighboring girls came almost every night to keep her company." Hoping that it might rid her of the persecution, Betsy was sent to the neighbors, "but it made no difference, the trouble followed her with the same severity, disturbing the family where she went as it did at home." But it is also significant to note that the Bell household was not "in any wise relieved" during Betsy's absence—as it should have been if she were the only cause of the manifestations.

By this time the mystery had gained wide notoriety; the house was crowded every night with visitors who persevered in their efforts to make the witch talk. They called on it "to rap on the wall, smack its mouth, etc." Finally, "it commenced whistling when spoken to, in a low, broken sound, as if trying to speak in a whistling voice, and in this way it progressed, developing until the whistling sound was changed to a weak, faltering whisper, uttering indistinct words. The voice, however, gradually gained strength in articulating, and soon the utterances became distinct in a low whisper, so as to be understood in the absence of any other noise."

This was a sensational development. The voice was not confined to darkness, as were the physical phenomena. "The talking was heard in lighted rooms as in the dark, and finally in the day at any hour." Some people accused Betsy of ventriloquism, so John, Jr., suggested a test to a visiting doctor. He placed his hand over Betsy's mouth at the time when the voice was heard and soon satisfied himself that she was in no way connected with the sounds.

Soon the witch was talking frequently, loudly, and, at first, piously. Naturally it was immediately asked to explain who it was, and a variety of answers were given. It loved to tease, and would say anything it thought would arouse its listeners. Once it said, "I am a Spirit from everywhere, Heaven, Hell, the Earth. I'm in the air, in houses, any place at any time. I've been created millions of years. That is all I will tell you."

Another time it declared, "I am a spirit; I was once very happy but have been disturbed." When asked to explain this it said, "I am the spirit of a person who was buried in the woods nearby, and the grave has been disturbed, my bones disinterred and scattered, and one of my teeth was lost under this house. I'm here looking for that tooth." Since an Indian burial ground had been found near the house when it was built and some of the bones had been discovered under the house, it seemed that this might possibly be true; and so a long and tiring hunt was begun for the lost tooth. It was never found, and the witch had a big laugh about it, declaring that it was all a trick to fool "Old Jack," as it called John Bell.

The witch sent the Bell boys on another wild goose chase when it said one day: "I am the spirit of an early immigrant, who brought a large sum of money and buried my treasure for safekeeping until needed. In the meanwhile I died without divulging the secret and I have returned in the spirit for the purpose of making known the hiding place. I want Betsy Bell to have the money."

Williams assures his readers that "The story was questioned and laughed at, and then discussed. The witch had made some remarkable revelations, and it was thought possible there might be something to it." It extracted promises and solemn oaths from the boys who would do the digging, that Betsy would get everything they found, and then it guided them to a spot in a field where there was a huge rock. Working terribly hard, they dug for hours until the rock was removed; and then, finding nothing, they dug farther for hours more, all to no avail. That night the spirit appeared to be in great glee, laughing and tantalizing the men for being so easily duped.

The description of itself that the entity gave which most suited the townspeople was that of a witch. Once somebody suggested that it must be a witch, and it seized that idea. "I am nothing more nor less than old Kate Batts' witch, and I'm determined to haunt and torment old Jack Bell as long as he lives," it said. Now Kate Batts was a well-known woman in the community who was the butt of many

jokes, and she had been dissatisfied in a business deal with John
Bell and had publicly threatened to "get" him. However, she was
very much alive and outlived John Bell by many years, so the idea
that she had anything to do with the thing was preposterous. She
was the wife of Frederick Batts, a hopeless cripple, and she had to
assume control of all the family business, which she had done very
successfully. But she was a large, fleshy woman, weighing well over
two hundred pounds. She was also headstrong, with a fearful tongue
and a bad temper, all of which had won her the name of "witch"
among the superstitious of her neighbors. However, she was actually
an enthusiastic Christian, always expounding on the Scripture and
the goodness of God. She also had an eccentric habit of putting on
extraordinary airs in an effort to appear elegant, and she used many
high-sounding bombastic words without knowing their proper mean-
ing. She was, therefore, the subject of much ridicule and had been
laughed at by the community for some years. When the voice said
it was old Kate Batts' witch, the idea caught on immediately; and
from then on everyone called the Bell Witch "Kate."

He, she, or it—the witch's sex was never actually divined—gained
a great reputation for religious piety at first. It called Mr. Johnson
"Old Sugar Mouth" because he prayed so sweetly. He was a lay
preacher and held services at his home which Kate loved to attend.
"Lord Jesus, how sweet Old Sugar Mouth prays; how I do love to
hear him," it observed frequently. Kate delighted in Scriptural
controversies, could quote any text or passage in the Bible (which
Betsy and the boys certainly were not able to do), and was able to
maintain a discussion with the ablest theologians who visited the
house, excelling in fervency of prayer and devotional songs. No
human voice was so charming.

Kate made frequent visits to North Carolina, John Bell's old
home state, never absent longer than a day, but always reporting
correctly the news or events in that vicinity when she returned.
With all these excellent traits of character, she still behaved badly
toward visitors and all members of the family except Mrs. Lucy
Bell, to whom she was devoted. She would declare that "Old Luce"
was a good woman; but she considered "Old Jack" to be most
detestable and loathsome. She often declared that it was her purpose
to kill him before leaving the place. Kate was also adverse to the
growing attachment between Joshua Gardner and Betsy Bell, and

remonstrated frequently, punishing Betsy severely in divers ways for receiving his devoted attentions.

Ingram describes a soft, melancholy voice, sighing in the distance and gradually approaching nearer with gentle pleadings in loud whispers: "Please, Betsy Bell, don't have Josh Gardner, please Betsy Bell, don't marry Josh Gardner." Ingram says, "It was so intensely persuasive, gentle and sweet, so extremely mystifying that it not only bewildered the lovers but brought perplexity and confusion into every social circle."

As time passed, the witch's remonstrations grew sharper and sharper. It "said so many things to Betsy and Joshua in the presence of their friends of a highly embarrassing nature that the girl in time became quite hysterical and worn out in despair." The witch insisted to John, Jr., that if Betsy married Joshua she would never have a day of happiness or peace.

Kate pried into everybody's business and domestic affairs in the community, as well as at the Bell home. She knew about every ludicrous thing that happened, and all the sordid, avaricious meanness that transpired; "divining the inmost secrets of the human heart, and withal, was a great blabbermouth, getting neighbors by the ears, taunting people with their sins and shortcomings, and laughing at their folly in trying to discover the identity of the mystery." However, she held fast to Christianity, and was a regular fire-eating Methodist while associating with "Old Sugar Mouth" and his sons. She regularly attended Mr. Johnson's prayer meetings, calling the "Amens," thumping on the chairs, and uttering the exclamation "Lord Jesus" frequently.

People now concluded that a good spirit had been sent to the community to work wonders and prepare the good at heart for the second advent. As fads do, the sensation spread hundreds of miles and people wild with excitement traveled long distances on horseback or in carriages and wagons to witness the demonstrations. Bell's home was continually overflowing with visitors and investigators of the phenomena. John Bell's hospitality, however, was equal to the great strain. He fed all visitors free of charge.

Citizens of the community learned to respect Kate's advice, as they also feared and abominated her scorpion tongue. So everybody suddenly turned "good"; the wicked left off swearing, lying and whiskey drinking; the avaricious were careful not to lay hands on anything belonging to their neighbors, lest Kate might tell on them.

No extraordinary incident occurred in the town that the witch did not know about, and she would immediately publish the fact. Whatever else may be said of the Bell Witch, it evinced an exalted opinion and profound respect for an honest man.

Unfortunately for the salvation of Kate's lost soul, she once attempted to take in the preaching of two ministers thirteen miles apart on the same day at the same hour, and "tried to mix the Methodist fire with Baptist water." This was too much for her. "It would perplex an angel, much less a presumptuous zealot, to run on both schedules at the same time," Ingram says. Kate succeeded to the extent of taking in both sermons; however, the mixture was too strong for her faith, and her whole stock of piety was lost in the transit. After this the witch backslid and fell from grace, took up with unregenerated spirits, held high carnival at John Gardner's still house, coming home very drunk, cursing and fussing, filling the house with bad breath, spitting on the Negroes, overturning the chairs, stripping the covers from the beds, pinching and slapping the children, and teasing Betsy in every conceivable way.

It was at this time of her retrogression that Kate introduced her family—and a sorry lot they were. There were sounds and evidence of other invisible entities about the place for some long time after that. Their names, they said, were Blackdog, who seemed to be the head of the family and spoke in a harsh feminine voice; Mathematics and Cypocryphy, whose voices were different, both more delicate feminine tones; and Jerusalem, who spoke like a boy. They all used obscene language, uttered vile threats, and made the night hideous with their drunken revelry. "On one occasion all four sounded almost beastly drunk, talking in maudlin sentimental strain, fuming the house with the scent of whiskey."

At the time that the witch's family was making the scene, Elizabeth went on a visit to her sister's house one day. During the afternoon, Esther started across the lane to gather up the eggs. Just as she passed from the yard into the road, she observed a woman walking slowly up the lane. She did not respond to Esther's greeting, as a neighbor would have done. But she took off her bonnet and let her hair down and began to comb it as she walked, apparently deeply absorbed or troubled. Esther talked to her, inviting her into the house, but the woman paid no attention. Esther showed the woman to Betsy and they both watched her for some time as she climbed on the yard fence and sat there for about five minutes, still combing away. Then she tucked up her hair, put on her sunbonnet, and walked over into the stable lot, where she could not possibly have had any business. After that three other persons appeared, two younger women or girls, and a boy. Each one bent down a sapling and then sat on them, riding them up and down, a popular game with the young of that day.

While this was going on Bennett Porter returned home, to find Esther and Elizabeth excited over the strange visitors, which they tried to point out to him. Although he could see the saplings bobbing up and down in an unnatural way, Bennett could not see the people the girls described. He suggested that they might be the apparitions of the witch's family, and went into the house and got his gun. He insisted that Esther should shoot them, because she could see them and he couldn't. Esther refused to shoot, but directed her husband's aim. The bullet cut the bark on the log where an apparition had been sitting, and at that moment they all disappeared. If they had been made of flesh and blood, so many people could not have escaped from the lot without detection. But there was no sign of them left, except for the bent saplings. At the Bell home that night the witch family made much ado about it, declaring to the company present that Bennett Porter had shot at Jerusalem and broken his arm with the bullet.

When the witch manifested out-of-doors, it was not uncommon to see lights like a candle or lamp flitting across the yard and through the fields. Frequently when John, his sons, and the Negro field hands were coming in late from work, chunks of wood and stones would fall along the way, as if tossed by someone. Williams asked William Porter, whom he describes as a very prominent citizen and a gentleman of high integrity, to tell about his own experiences with this. William Porter related that he used to go to school with Joel Bell and, returning in the evening, the boys would pass some briar patches and hazel thickets by the wayside. At this spot, Porter says, "sticks of wood and rocks were often tossed to us, but never with much force, and we soon learned not to fear any harm from this pastime, and frequently cut notches on the sticks, casting them back into the thicket from whence they came, and invariably the same sticks would be hurled back at us."

As if to refute the objection that the boys might have been the victims of a practical joke, at night the witch would recount everything that had happened to them along the way. "Even if one of us stumped a toe, falling over, the witch claimed to have caused it, and would describe how she appeared in the form of a rabbit or something else at a certain place."

William Porter had another witch story. He said that one night as he settled down to bed in the cabin in which he lived alone, he heard the unmistakable voice of Kate. "Billy, I have come to sleep with you and keep you warm." He replied, "Well, Kate, if you are going to sleep with me, you must behave yourself." She did not behave herself, however:

"The cover continued to slip in spite of my tenacious grasp, and was twisted into a roll on the back side of the bed, just like a boy would roll himself in a quilt, and not a strip was left on me. I jumped out of bed in a second, and observing that the witch had rolled up in the cover, the thought struck me: 'I have got you now, you rascal, and will burn you up.' In an instant I grabbed the roll of cover in my arms and started to the fire, intending to throw the cover, witch and all, in the blaze. I discovered that it was very weighty and smelled awful. I had not got halfway across the room before the luggage got so heavy and became so offensive that I was compelled to drop it on the floor and rush out of doors for a breath of fresh air. The odor emitted from the roll was the most offensive stench I ever smelled. It was absolutely stifling, and I could not have endured it another second. After being refreshed, I returned to the room and gathered up the roll of bed clothing, shook them out, but the witch had departed and there was no unusual weight or offensive odor remaining; and this is just how near I came to catching the witch."

Richard Williams Bell tells how his sister was "subjected to fainting spells followed by prostration, characterized by shortness of breath and smothering sensations, panting as it were for life, and becoming entirely exhausted and lifeless, losing her breath for nearly a minute between gasps, and rendered unconscious. These spells lasted from thirty to forty minutes, and passed off as suddenly, leaving her perfectly restored after a few minutes, in which she recovered from the exhaustion. There is no positive evidence that these spells were produced by the witch. However, that was the conclusion from the fact that no other cause was apparent. She is a very stout girl and, with this exception, the personification of robust health, and was never subject to hysteria or anything of the kind. Moreover, the spells came on at regular hours in the evening, just at the time the witch usually appeared, and immediately after the spells passed off the mysterious voice commenced talking, but never uttered a word during the time of prostration." Williams did not know, of course, that these spells of Betsy's resemble mediumistic trances; but if they were such, there is little doubt but that she was being used to supply power for the ghostly, and ghastly, activities. Certain types of mediums are able to produce from their bodies a usually invisible substance called ectoplasm which, it is alleged, spirit entities use to produce their phenomena.

Williams also mentions that his father suffered from peculiar spells, of a different nature. In fact, "his ailment commenced with the incipiency of the witch's demonstration, or before he recognized the phenomenal disturbances. He complained of a curious sensational feeling in his mouth, a stiffness of the tongue, and something like a stick cross-wise, punching each side of his jaws. As time went on this affliction increased, his tongue swelling against his jaws so that he could neither talk nor eat for ten or fifteen hours at a time."

The suffering of John Bell was funny to no one but the witch, who had quite a distorted sense of humor. One of its pranks does amuse, however, even though it must have been very disagreeable to poor Betsy. Mr. Ingram interviewed Mrs. Lucinda E. Rawls, who had been one of Betsy's intimate girl friends. It seems that a witch doctor came to town insisting that he could rid Betsy of Kate's spell if she would take his medicine. Mrs. Rawls is quoted about the incident as follows:

"Mother remonstrated with Betsy against taking the awful dose, but she persisted that she would take anything that anybody would give her, if it was poison, to get rid of her excruciating pest, and so she did swallow it down. It very soon made her deathly sick, as the conjurer promised it would." She threw up, and when the vomit was examined it was "found to be literally full of pins and needles, and Kate, the witch, fairly roared with laughter, and said that fellow was the only conjurer who had ever done any good; he had made Betsy throw up pins and needles enough to supply the whole community, and if he would give her another dose of the stuff she would get enough to set up a pin-and-needle store. The witch doctor really believed that the pins and needles were ejected from the girl's stomach, and was astounded by the result of his own practice. There could be no mistake that they were real brass pins and needles. Mother gathered up a number and kept them as long as she lived. I have seen the pins and needles myself. As a matter of course, Betsy could not have lived with such a conglomeration in her stomach, and the only solution of the matter was that the witch dropped in the pins and needles unobserved."

The witch had a weakness for pins, it seems, as we read further on that pins were frequently found in the bed pillows, stuck from the inside of the pillow-case with points out, and sometimes found in the chairs. They were frequently stuck into poor Betsy as well.

Poltergeists often produce odd objects of mysterious origin, in an unknown way, apparently from thin air. They are similar to the "apports" produced by some physical mediums. Kate was no exception. She participated in Mrs. Bell's Bible study meetings and when refreshments were served would bring in nice fruits for the guests, simply dropping them on the table or into the laps of the visitors. At Betsy's birthday party the witch called out, "I have a surprise for you; come and see it." And there, placed on the table by unseen hands, was a large basket of fruit—oranges, bananas, grapes, and nuts—such things as were seldom in the stores in those days. Kate called out, "Those came from the West Indies. I brought them myself."

When Mrs. Bell fell ill, Kate was disconsolate. She claimed no power to heal and was as helpless in the face of illness as a child. Her plaintive voice could be heard exclaiming, "Luce, poor Luce, how do you feel now? Hold out your hands, Luce, and I'll give you something." Hazelnuts were then dropped into Lucy's outstretched palms. When she didn't eat them because they were not cracked, the witch threw cracked nuts onto her lap. There were several visitors present at the time, and they made a great to-do about examining the ceiling to see if there was a hole large enough for the nuts to have dropped through, but they found nothing of the sort.

In both books about the witch a good bit of evidence is presented that it could forecast the weather, that it was free from spatial limitations, and that it had telepathic and clairvoyant powers. One night, for instance, Lucy Bell came into the sitting room and inquired if anyone knew whether her son Jesse, who lived a mile away, had returned from a business trip. The voice of Kate was heard saying, "Wait a minute, Luce, I'll go and see for you." Scarcely a minute later she returned, reporting that Jesse was at home, sitting at a table reading by the light of a candle. Jesse said later that the account was accurate, and that at the time he had heard a distinct rap and had seen the door open and close, although no one visible was there.

Kate frequently offered to help the Bell family with good advice, but they usually disregarded it. One Sunday evening, shortly after the witch had found her voice, the family was discussing a proposed trip of John, Jr.'s, to North Carolina to look after his father's interests in an estate that was to be settled. Kate entered the conversation saying, "You'll have trouble. You'll have the trip for nothing. The estate has not been settled and won't be for some time. You'll get no money." It then offered the further information that an elegant young lady was on her way from Virginia to visit friends in Robertson County, that she was wealthy, "possessing forty Negroes," and that, if he would stay, he could win her. Young John just laughed, and left the next morning. Over six months later he returned empty-handed. In the meantime, the girl described had arrived soon after his departure, and had left before his return, and so John never met her.

The witch never seems to have presented visible shape to anyone except on the one occasion when Betsy and Esther saw its whole family; but the evidence clearly suggests that it had a body which, though invisible, was of solid, palpable substance. Those in whom Kate had confidence could feel a soft and velvety hand like a woman's slipping into their extended palms, but those who aroused her ire could feel a hand with blows falling fast and heavy.

In a local cave nearby, now known as the "Bell Witch Cave" and famous for its stalactites, one of Betsy's boy friends got into a bad situation one day. He had to get down on his knees to crawl and became jammed in a quicksand deposit. His candle went out, and no one could get to him to help him. "Suddenly the big room and all parts of the cave were lit up as if from a big lamp. A voice called out, 'I'll get you out.' The boy's legs were seized as if by strong hands and he was drawn out with his face full of mud and nearly suffocated."

As has been said, John Bell never accepted pay for boarding any of the people who came to see the witch, and a bed and a meal was always ready for everyone. But when General Andrew Jackson—he had not yet become President of the United States—came from Nashville to learn if the stories he had heard about the witch were true, he had no intention of imposing on the Bells. His party rode on horseback accompanied by a wagon loaded with a tent and ample provisions so that they could camp on the property. In his company was a man who claimed to be a "witch-layer," a profession that was not unpopular in the early nineteenth century. As they neared the Bell farm they were joking about the proper procedures for laying a ghost when the wagon stopped suddenly, stuck fast in its tracks. The driver lashed the horses, but they were not able to budge an inch. Jackson ordered the men on horseback to dismount and put their shoulders to the wheel, but the wagon still would not move. Suddenly it dawned on the General. Throwing up his hands, he exclaimed, "By the Eternal, it's the witch!"

Just then a voice came from the bushes beside the road, saying, "All right, General, let the wagon move on. I'll see you again tonight." And then the horses started off of their own accord, and the wagon rolled ahead.

At the Bell home, where he was warmly received, Jackson decided to sit up with the witch-layer and the others and wait for the haunt to make itself evident. In the dark room, lighted only by one tallow candle, the witch-layer rambled on and on about his prowess. He was a brawny man with long hair, black mustache and high cheekbones, and he sat with a flintlock horse pistol on his lap. He explained that it was loaded with a silver bullet, which was necessary if one wanted to eliminate a witch. Recounting numerous instances in which he had been successful, he bored the company to death. He had once shot a cat with a silver bullet, he said, while it was sitting on the coffin of a bewitched woman. He showed the cat's tail, which he carried for good luck.

Jackson began to yawn and twist about in his chair. Finally he whispered to the man nearest him, "I bet that fellow's a coward. I wish the witch would come. I'd like to see him run."

The witch came. There was a noise like dainty footsteps prancing on the bare floor, quickly followed by the same voice they had heard from the bushes. "All right, General, I'm on hand ready for business." Then it said to the witch-layer, "Now, Mr. Smarty, here I am. Shoot!"

The man stroked his nose with the cat's tail, leveled his pistol at the place where the voice had been heard, and pulled the trigger. But the gun failed to fire.

"Try again," Kate gloated, but again there was no result. "Now it's my turn," came the voice. "Look out, you old coward, you hypocrite, you fraud. I'll teach you a lesson."

Ingram says, "The next thing a sound was heard like that of boxing with the open hand, whack, whack, and the oracle tumbled over like lightning had struck him, but he quickly recovered his feet and went capering around the room like a frightened steer, running over everyone in his way, yelling, 'Oh, my nose, my nose, the devil has got me. Oh, lordy, he's got me by the nose.' Suddenly, as if by its own accord, the door flew open and the witch-layer dashed out, and made a beeline for the lane at full speed, yelling every jump. Everybody rushed out under the excitement, expecting the man would be killed, but as far as they could hear up the lane, he was still running and yelling." Jackson, they say, dropped to the ground and rolled over and over laughing.

"By the Eternal, boys, I never saw so much fun in all my life," he said. Presently the witch returned and joined in the laughter. Old Hickory was anxious to stay a week, but his party had had enough, and no inducement could keep them.

Except for Josh, Old Kate was partial to those Betsy liked and hostile to those she disliked. John, Jr., was Betsy's favorite brother and the witch never abused him. But it was ever ready to show a frightful temper toward most others, excepting always Lucy, whom it declared to be "the most perfect woman living." Joel and Williams were often thrashed. Drewry lived in such fear of the witch that he never married, living a secluded bachelor's life under the apprehension that the witch would visit some dreadful calamity on him.

It is little wonder that he was so afraid, after what he saw Kate do to his father. John's spells continually got worse and worse. His face jerked and twitched, and his tongue became so swollen that his whole face appeared distorted. Each spell would last from one to two days, as the witch grew ever angrier at him and more virulent in its attacks. During one severe spell, which confined John Bell to his bed for six or seven days, the witch cursed and raved like a maniac and never ceased troubling him. After he got better, he was attacked in the open air one day. His shoes were repeatedly jerked off, a phenomenon to which Richard Williams bears personal witness:

"Presently he complained of a blow on his face which felt like an open hand that almost stunned him, and he sat down on a log that lay by the roadside. Then his face commenced jerking with fearful contortions. Soon his whole body; and then his shoes would fly off as fast as I could put them on. The situation was trying and made me shudder. I was terrified by the spectacle of the contortions that seized Father, as if to convert him into a very demon to swallow me up. Having finished tying Father's shoes, I raised myself up to hear the reviling sound of derisive songs piercing the air with terrorizing force. As the demoniac shrieks died away in triumphant rejoicing, the spell passed off and I saw tears chasing down Father's yet quivering cheeks."

On returning to the house, John Bell said, "My son, this terrible thing is killing me. I feel that the end is nigh." Then he looked up and prayed that this affliction might pass. He took to his bed that day and declined rapidly from then on. Nothing that anybody could do helped him. Dr. George Hopson of Port Royal was called and gave him various medications, but all to no avail.

On December 19, 1820, John Bell was discovered in a deep stupor and could not be aroused. John, Jr., went to the medicine cupboard where he always carefully kept his father's prescriptions; but instead of the bottle for which he was looking he found "a smoky looking vial, which was about one-third full of dark colored liquid." Dr. Hopson was sent for immediately, and when he arrived he was accompanied by various neighbors. They all heard the witch in joyous exultation: "It's useless for you to try to revive Old Jack. I've got him this time. He'll never get up from that bed again!" Asked about the vial of medicine found in the cupboard, Kate replied: "I put it there and gave Old Jack a big dose out of it last night while he was fast asleep, which fixed him."

The doctor suggested that a test be made of the contents of the vial. A straw was run into it and wiped on the tongue of a cat. "The cat jumped and whirled over a few times, stretched out, kicked and died very quick." The bottle and contents were thrown into the fire, and instantly a blue haze shot up the chimney like a flash of powder.

John Bell died the following morning. Kate was around during the time, indulging in wild exultations and derisive songs. At the burial "after the grave was filled and the friends turned to leave the sad scene, the witch broke out in a loud voice, singing 'Row me up some brandy, O,' and continued singing this until the family and friends had all entered the house."

With the killing of John Bell the witch had attained one of its goals. Its other declared intent was to keep Betsy from marrying Josh Gardner. By now the girl was fifteen years old, and had ripened into lovely young womanhood. Even though she was so often accused by strangers of having perpetrated the witch hoax, she was popular with her friends and the members of her community, and known for her extraordinary beauty and winsome ways. An old resident of the area, Mrs. Mahala Darden, described her to Ingram as a lovely girl, blonde, with a graceful figure and elegant carriage. "She possessed a rare suit of rich golden hair, soft, gentle blue eyes, and winning ways, and with all was an industrious, bright and interesting girl, who had more admirers than any girl in the county. I thought a great deal of Betsy; she was a sweet, good girl, and I deeply sympathized with her in her disappointments and afflictions."

Betsy had been made very unhappy by her father's death; but as time passed her grief gradually was assuaged. Also, it became evident that with her father's passing the witch had relaxed its persecutions of her to a considerable extent. As she was teased and mauled less and less by her invisible enemy she began to dream that her hopes might be fulfilled after all. Finally, on Easter Sunday, she and Josh announced their engagement, and she proudly showed her ring to her friends. It was on a picnic and fishing trip to celebrate this engagement that Kate returned in full force, playing tricks with the fish to the extent that nobody caught anything that day, and the Negro servants all got a good ducking. Then the soft, melancholy voice of the witch came again, as it had so often in the past, "Please, Betsy Bell, don't marry Josh Gardner."

Then it was that Betsy realized it was no use to hope. She had heard the warnings so often, and she was sure that if she married Josh neither of them would ever be free of the witch's curse. It was clear that it would follow her through life, torturing and teasing. She and Joshua might even be killed as her father had been. No, she could not wish such a life on her beloved. Betsy summoned the courage to hand Josh back his ring and break the engagement. He took it with his usual good manners, expressing the fact that although his heart was broken, he knew that she had acted in good faith and had done what she believed to be right. Even with the bitter anguish the forsaken lover endured, there is just the slightest possibility that he was somewhat relieved to be let out of such an uncomfortable situation.

Oddly enough, the schoolmaster, Professor Richard Powell, had returned to town and put in an appearance at that same picnic. During the years that the witch had been at the height of its activity, he had been in Springfield, as a State Representative. He was many years Betsy's senior, but was a "handsome gentleman who bore an honorable name and reputation. He was prominent in public affairs and one of the most popular men in Robertson County." He became a persistent suitor as soon as Betsy's engagement to Joshua was broken; and, since the witch had no objection to him, they eventually were married.

The married life of Betsy and Dick Powell was relatively short —about seventeen years—when Powell died. Betsy remained a widow for the rest of her life, dying at the age of eighty-six. As she got older she fulfilled the promise of her baby fat, and became a very stout woman. She was high-spirited, and noted throughout her life for her industrious habits, good nature, and splendid social qualities, being always entertaining in any circle, Ingram says. She bore the harassment of her early life with great fortitude, even though the misrepresentation of her role in the Bell Witch's activities continually plagued her.

When Betsy broke her engagement to Josh Gardner she also broke the witch's hold on the family. It had no more reason to stay around, and it gradually made itself felt less and less. The final phenomenon took place as the family was sitting around the fire after their evening meal. "Something like a cannonball rolled down the chimney and out into the room, bursting like a smoke ball. A voice clearly called out, 'I am going, and will be gone for seven years. Goodbye to all.' "

The promise to return in seven years was fulfilled. By then Mrs. Bell, Joel and Williams were the only occupants of the homestead. Betsy was married to Dick Powell. The manifestations when they reappeared consisted of scratching sounds and the pulling off of the bedcovers. Williams writes: "We decided not to speak to it and to keep the matter a profound secret. It kept up its disturbances about two weeks and then left forever." Williams adds that this was his last experience with Kate.

But during the time it was around, the witch also paid two visits to the home of John, Jr. There it spoke, and promised to return again in 107 years. At that time, it said, it would be the bearer of evil tidings for Tennessee and the whole nation.

After this, from time to time over the next fifty years, various people of the village claimed to see evidence of Kate's activities. The area around the Bell house, even when the house itself was torn down and moved away, was said to be haunted; and many people claimed to see lights and other manifestations. None of the Bell family ever did, however.

Williams concludes his diary by wondering why it all had to happen in the first place. "John Bell had lived in peace, and in the enjoyment of the full confidence of his neighbors, and lacked not for scores of friends in his severest trials. Then why this infliction? Where the cause?" What exactly *could* have been back of it all? He answers, "We, who experienced or witnessed the demonstration, know there was a wonderful power of intelligence, possessing knowledge of men and things, a spirit of divination, that could read minds, tell men's secrets, quote the Scriptures, repeat sermons, sing hymns and songs, assume bodily forms, and with all, an immense physical force behind the manifestations."

The witch had been investigated thoroughly by everyone who heard anything about it and who wished to see it. The Bells had always allowed visitors and any kind of probes. Besides local citizens, hundreds of men from other communities visited the place, remaining for days and nights, for the same purpose. All failed in the object of detecting the cause of the demonstrations. "People followed every clue, exercised all of their wits, applied all manner of tests, placed unsuspected detectives in and around the house, acted upon all suggestions regarding the suspicion that had been lodged against certain members of the family, and with all their investigations ended in confusion, leaving the affair shrouded in still deeper mystery, which no one to this day has ever been able to account for or explain in any intelligent or satisfactory way."

1935 would have been the 107th year, on which Kantankerous Kate's promised return was scheduled. But 1935 came and went with no sign of her. Descendants of John Bell heaved justifiable sighs of relief.

CHAPTER FIFTEEN

THE OLD STRAW PLACE

THE OLD STRAW PLACE in Newfield, Maine, was not built *of* straw, but *by* Straw—Gideon Straw, Esq., circa 1787. His daughter Hannah haunts it—and with good reason. She is buried there in the house.

It is not very often that a tombstone can be found right in the corner of a kitchen floor. In fact, this is probably the only house extant that has a burial marker as a built-in feature. The marker is a metal plate about five feet long and two feet wide, shaped exactly like a headstone, but laid flat. It had been bricked into the floor, and in recent years it has been cemented around to keep dirt from coming up through the cracks. Still, it could do with the addition of a blanket of grass and some flowers to make it into a really respectable burial plot. If I were Hannah I'd haunt a house, too, whose occupants did no better by my grave than that.

The text of the inscription reads:

> Sacred to the memory of Hannah, Wife of Ira Chadbourne,
> Who died March 2, 1826. Age 30.
> Blest are the dead, who die in Christ,
> Whose triumph is so great,
> Who calmly wait a nobler life,
> A nobler life shall meet.

Over the top of a willow tree is etched. This means, to students of tombstones, that the person buried there died young. Since the family graveyard nearby also has a duplicate plaque dedicated to the memory of Hannah Chadbourne, the question rises as to whether she is buried there or in the house. But the evidence of large slabs of rock shaped like a coffin and lying in the basement directly under the area where the metal plate is, would seem to indicate that the body is in the house.

In some ancient homes in New England flat boards have been found that are the length of a human body and shaped somewhat like surfboards. They were used in the old days when someone died in the middle of winter and the ground was frozen too solid for a grave to be dug. The deceased was fastened securely to the board and placed in the attic to chill thoroughly until spring. After the first thaw he was ceremoniously, and quickly, buried. Perhaps a similar situation existed on the cold, early March day when Hannah died. Perhaps the ground was so solidly frozen that year that she could not be buried outside, so she was put under the floor in the kitchen. And because she had been so securely and tidily laid to rest, it was probably decided to leave her there, and a memorial plaque placed in the cemetery in her honor.

But if her family did not want to disturb poor Hannah, she has no qualms about disturbing others. Whether or not her body is in that house, her spirit certainly is, according to some who have lived there. Darrell McLaughlin is the one who probably had the most unpleasant encounters with Hannah. In partnership with two other men, he bought the house in 1958 to be used as a hunting lodge. There was quite a bit of drinking going on from time to time, as is often the case with hunting parties; and a tradition grew up somehow to end each evening with a toast to Hannah. As these sometimes inebriated men stood about the grave and laughingly saluted her, Hannah must have resented it, and not unreasonably—at least, Darrell McLaughlin began to think so.

A man with a conscience, even when he'd had a few, Darrell would lie in bed afterward and think about Hannah, and wonder how he would have liked it if his tombstone had been in the kitchen of a house where a lot of scrubby hunters were making fun of it. Especially after his health began to fail, and he would lie abed with aches and pains, McLaughlin would concentrate on Hannah and feel sorry for her. It was about that time that he bought out his two partners and lived in the house alone.

I know you are going to think it was because he was alone and not feeling well and was terribly impressionable that Darrell McLaughlin began to see Hannah. But I'm not so sure. Perhaps, instead, because she was now able to get through to him, she showed herself.

Anyway, it got so that along about 11:10 every night Darrell would see Hannah at the window that opened from the kitchen shed into the large room where he sat. He would leave the room quickly and jump into the safety of his bed and pull the covers up around his ears. This helped, at first. Then, getting more nerve, Hannah began coming into his bedroom and leaning over his bed and stroking his cheek. He could not see her, but he felt her. He let her get by with it for a brief period, but there was no telling what she might try if she were becoming that bold. So he sold the house. It was the only safe thing for him to do.

Darrell McLaughlin was perfectly fair, though. He told the young schoolteachers who bought the place exactly what his experiences had been and why he was leaving. Russell Fairbanks and Robert Drafahl were not in the least deterred by what they heard. In fact, they were encouraged to buy the house, for they thought it would be fun to own a ghost.

They had always wanted an old colonial home which they could spend their summers restoring, and getting one with the extra dividend of a built-in haunt was even more than they had hoped for. Although the place was rundown, and they have not had the time to do much to improve it, they have delighted in its evidences of antiquity—the French wallpaper in the front room dating from 1820; the original wallpaper in the hall put on in squares instead of strips, which, they say, means that it was made before 1800; the plaster walls. Russell told me that, while paneling is now a sign of luxury, plaster walls were the In thing at the time this house was built. Obviously Gideon Straw, who had started out in the records when he bought the property as "laborer," became a "gentleman" after he built the house. Only a gentleman could have afforded such things as plaster walls. With the added status that owning such a sumptuous residence gave to his dignity, Gideon Straw added "Esquire" to his name on the bill of sale when he later sold the house to his son Daniel.

But what the house did for Gideon Straw it obviously did not do for McLaughlin or for the young teachers who now own it. They have accepted positions to teach in Florida, and the house is once again up for sale.

Russell Fairbanks told me about his only unusual experience there, which, although quite peculiar, did not seem to involve Hannah. What it did involve, he has no idea. One night during the Easter weekend, 1966, he was asleep in an upstairs room when he heard a door open and heavy footsteps go across the floor downstairs right below him. He knew this could hardly be Bob or their guest, for they did not make that much noise. "So," he said, "I sat up on the edge of the bed and got my gun out of the drawer of a nearby table. And then I woke up!" There he was sitting on the edge of the bed with the gun in his hand, but he had evidently been dreaming. "It must have been a dream," he said. "What else could it have been? I very definitely had the feeling of waking up, yet there I was on the edge of the bed with the gun in my hand."

Russell and Robert heard a great deal of noise in the house from time to time that at first they could not account for. Naturally they always attributed it to Hannah, until they discovered what it really was. They learned that much of the strange racket was caused by swallows in their chimneys. Now there is no doubt that these birds can make an awful noise in the wide fireplace chimneys of old houses. But it sounds like only one thing—birds in chimneys, not ghosts. However, if you were listening for a Hannah to make her presence known at any moment, perhaps you could delude yourself briefly.

The young teachers also heard a most spectacular roaring and banging, which awoke them with a start on a cold winter night. "Poltergeists!" they thought. But nothing so spectacular could be blamed. When the same thing occurred the next morning, they realized that it was snow and ice falling off their roof.

"Ma" Sweeney, who once lived in the old Straw place, is now eighty-nine years old and lives in West Newfield. She has been called "Ma" by everyone in the community for so long that she almost forgets that she was originally named Martha Louise. Mrs. Sweeney said that when she lived in the house the kitchen stove was placed right on top of the slab which contained the tombstone, and she did not know the grave was there. During the entire time she lived in the house she never saw Hannah's ghost nor heard it.

"But, you know," she said, "there was one real funny thing that happened. The night my daughter-in-law died in the house there was a terrible whining noise coming up through all the fireplaces."

Ma Sweeney said emphatically, "Of course, it was probably the wind. We all said that." And yet—there was not much wind blowing at all that night. And they never heard that remarkable, piercing, frightening noise at any other time than just on that one occasion when Mrs. Sweeney's daughter-in-law died. "Yes," said Ma, "that was really very strange, very strange."

Many old ghost houses seem to have stories about buried money. I have run into several here and there in my search, although I have never met anyone who claimed to have found any such hidden treasure. When Fairbanks and Drafahl went down to pay their taxes recently, they mentioned that they had learned from the previous owner and others that there was supposed to be money hidden in the house. The town clerk, Gertrude Mee, agreed that she also had heard that rumor all her life. She had lived in the area and knew its history, and had always heard that money was buried there. But she would not have dreamed of hunting for it. She told them, "When I was a little girl we wouldn't even walk past the old Straw house. It was always reputed to be haunted."

Anybody want to buy a haunted house?

CHAPTER SIXTEEN

THE GHOST
AT THE FOLLIES

SHE JUST STOOD THERE and looked at Benny—a slim auburn-haired girl, wearing a yellow sweater and a brown skirt. Possibly she might have been applying for a job in burlesque, Benny thought, except that the hour was 4:00 A.M. Then, again, perhaps she had come into the theater for protection.

"What can I do for you?" Benny asked the girl, but she did not answer. Instead, she turned and flitted away, and before he could get up and follow her she had disappeared. Benny searched the theater, but he could find no trace of her.

Benny Roberson, a young man who numbers among his other duties the job of night watchman at the Follies Theater in Los Angeles, had heard rumors of a ghost there. Now he is convinced that he has seen her in person. And he has experienced other weird and unaccountable things in the dilapidated old building where he works.

At the Follies, young girls with bare bodies and G-strings now contort in the latest dance gyrations on the stage where Paderewski once performed his great piano selections, and Mme. Schumann-Heinck's voice flowed forth in mellow musical magic. Some eighty years ago, this theater at 337 S. Main Street was known as the Belasco, the best theater in town. When Hollywood show business was in its infancy, W. C. Fields, Lewis Stone, Marjorie Rambeau, Hobart Bosworth, and many other movie immortals made personal appearances there. They would sigh to see the present rundown condition of the boards they once trod in glory. But would they bother to haunt the place?

Somebody haunts it though. Benny is not the only one to whom the specter has appeared. Strippers Fifi LaRue and Gogi Grey have also claimed the experience, according to William S. Taylor, the assistant manager of the Follies. Taylor has not seen the ghost himself, but he has heard plenty of stories about her. He agrees with Benny, who maintains that she is the spirit of a despondent stripper who hung herself in the basement of the building. These men tell of ropes that move of their own volition, and a vase that exploded.

The rows of ropes, which extend to the ceiling and raise and lower the stage backdrops, have been known to vibrate strongly when no one is near them. When they have begun swinging back and forth the men have tried to hold them, but have been unable to keep them still. Yet, if they are commanded to stop, the vibrations in the ropes cease immediately. To the people who work backstage at the Follies Theater, this is an indication that their haunt is swinging on the ropes. Does she, having ended her life on a rope, now have a strange affinity for hemp?

And did she also cause that vase to explode when Benny and Barbara deVere were alone in a dressing room having a chat? It was in August 1965, when this strange occurrence took place. Barbara, who is a stripper, is the daughter of the owner of the theater and the wife of the manager. She says there were no flowers or water in the green pottery vase. It was being used as an ashtray, actually. "Suddenly it just exploded!" she says with awe in her voice.

"It was the ghost!" Benny maintains, and no one can tell him differently. Not even Barbara's husband, who insists that he invented the ghost and that she is merely a figment of his and numerous other imaginations. A few years ago, he says, the narrow dressing rooms didn't have enough space to suit the girls and they began to complain. "Why don't you open up that other room?" they asked on many occasions, referring to a space at the far end of their dressing area that was always kept boarded up. The manager did not want to be bothered coping with one more room. It was bad enough as it was trying to get anybody to keep the place neat. (Cleaning thoroughly does not seem to be a custom of the Follies. Some of the dirt there now must date from the opening night of the Belasco Theater.) So he just told the girls he did not want to open that room because it was haunted.

"That's all it needed," he says. "Imagination did all the rest."

It isn't difficult for imagination to run wild in the dismal darkness backstage at this theater. And everyone knows, even if they have not personally climbed up the three narrow flights to see it, as I have, that there is a small room at the top of the building containing weird secrets. In a far corner high above the stage, across the catwalk—where one could step off abruptly into space, down through all the scenery flats and curtains to the stage itself—is a tiny, dark, musty room, piled high with ropes, rolls of canvas, and junk that has accumulated over the years along with dust and grime. Once this room belonged to a scene painter who worked and lived in the theater. He had the curious habit of papering his walls with pictures and newspaper clippings about burlesque showgirls.

What's unusual about a man collecting girlie pictures? He saved only pictures and clippings about the girls who had died or been killed, or committed suicide! This man, whose name is forgotten in the antiquity of the theater, is remembered only for the torn remnants relating countless tragic moments, dried and yellowing pieces of paper rotting away on the walls of his room. Perhaps if it were possible to spend long enough with these fusty relics, one could find a clipping that tells of a particular girl who hung herself in the basement of the Follies Theater.

No talk of imagination is going to convince Johnnie Lattimore that he has not seen a real spook. In fact, he swears that he had never heard the rumors about a ghost there the first time he saw her. Johnnie, who lives at 2501 4th Avenue in Los Angeles, is a short, stocky individual of twenty-five, who looks like what he prefers to be known as, a professional fighter. He has worked at the Follies for the past three years, but only as a fill-in between his fighting engagements. At first he cleaned up at the theater, then he began to work backstage. Now, he very competently handles the lights, music, backdrops, and the timing of each act—getting the girls on and off stage with precision. Johnnie is a no-nonsense type, and one tends to want to believe him when he says he had glimpses of the ghost not once but five times. He first saw her, he says, in May or June 1965, and he last saw her just two or three weeks before he was telling this tale—in October 1965.

As the records play and the near-nude girls twist and writhe on-stage, Johnnie Lattimore talks about the apparition he has seen in this theater.

"She wears a white negligee," he says. "Always a white negligee." The first time he saw her she was running toward the staircase that twists upward toward the dressing rooms and the catwalk at the top of the stage. He bounded up the stairs after her, to remove this stranger from the theater where she had no business to be. But he never caught up with her. She had disappeared in the tortuous twists of the circular stairway.

The second time Johnnie saw her she was at the third landing, with her arms on the railing, her chin leaning on her hands. She was staring down at him with an intense, though not malevolent, gaze. Johnnie once again raced up the stairs to catch her. He was not as shocked now at her appearance, because after telling people about his earlier peculiar experience, he had been informed about the ghost. Not one to be afraid of the unknown, Johnnie has been merely interested and curious the several times since then when he has seen the swishing skirt of her negligee. Once he heard only her footsteps in the otherwise empty theater. Another time he heard her steps behind him as he was going out the door. Turning quickly to look back, he glimpsed the flipping tip of her skirts as she retreated. These last experiences were not so impressive, but the first two times he saw her are engraved on his brain forever.

"She looked real to me," Johnnie Lattimore says. "She had sandy-red hair, and she was right pretty. Her face was smooth and round." But she could not have been real. She *must* have been a ghost, because she never was there when he reached the place where she should have been.

"She'd just disappeared," says Johnnie. "Vanished!"

CHAPTER SEVENTEEN

LINDENWALD
NEAR KINDERHOOK

AARON BURR REALLY GOT AROUND. During his lifetime, that is. Whether or not he still gets around in the various haunted houses with which he seems to be connected is something for conjecture. But there are those who tie him in rather conclusively with the haunting of Lindenwald.

Lindenwald is a charming old house just south of the town of Kinderhook in Columbia County, about twenty miles below Albany, New York. The curious word "Kinderhook" is Dutch for "children's corner," and must have had a certain significance for the many prolific Dutch settlers of this section of the state. The whole area is redolent with Washington Irving: he visited there often; he knew the local schoolmaster, on whose career he based his Ichabod Crane character; and he tutored the grandchildren of Judge Van Ness, who built Lindenwald. Irving's "Legend of Sleepy Hollow," while not exactly putting Kinderhook on the map, lent it many colorful characteristics, such as the Ichabod Crane School and the Van Allen house, where the earthly prototype of Katrina Van Tassel lived.

It was Martin Van Buren who gave Kinderhook lasting fame. The eighth President of the United States was born there in 1782. A short, handsome, red-haired man who was very popular with his constituents, he held more public offices than any other president ever has. He also owned Lindenwald, and for all we know it might be his footsteps that have been heard in the old house on so many occasions since then.

But it is more likely to be Aaron Burr, who had many more sins on his conscience, and should therefore be much more prone to haunt houses.

Lindenwald was built in 1797 by Judge William Peter Van Ness.

It was, at first, merely a solid, typical, well-balanced, brick Dutch farmhouse of the post-colonial period; but even from the beginning, it seemed destined for an exciting career. The Judge's son William, known to all as "Billy," was Aaron Burr's second in the famous duel in which Alexander Hamilton was killed. Dueling had already become a bit *déclassé* in this country, and Alexander Hamilton was a tremendously popular man—much better liked than egotistical little rabble-rouser Burr. Therefore, after the duel it seemed genuine good sense for Burr to disappear, and this he did for a period of three years. Where did he hide during this time? Was it Lindenwald? There is interesting new evidence tending to confirm this, which will be presented in its chronological sequence.

When Martin Van Buren retired from the presidency, he was ready to settle down in his old home town. Having once studied law under Judge Van Ness, he was a friend of the family's, and he prevailed upon Billy to sell him Lindenwald. Nine years later he hired the famous architect Richard Upjohn, who had just completed Trinity Church in New York City, to remodel the house. The original square structure was enlarged with wings on the south and west. A steep front gable was added, and a rococo porch, scalloped cornices, and an Italian campanile-type bell tower. Van Buren imported many articles to make the interior as elaborate as the rest. In the parlor he hung wallpaper depicting a huge painting. He had Italian marble fireplaces of a different color installed in each room, and numerous Brussels carpets of warm red and yellow shades.

Lindenwald has been remodeled several times since Van Buren's day, and the present owner, Kenneth Campbell, has added a large veranda across the front which seems to put everything back into its proper perspective. Campbell, incidentally, has not seen or heard a single ghostly phenomenon during his ten-year tenure. Today the house is not open to the public, although it has been from time to time in the past. Mr. and Mrs. Campbell live there quietly and run an antique shop in the gatehouse. But it is to be hoped that some day the old mansion will be turned into a historical monument and the furniture and paraphernalia of the early days restored as much as possible to their original state.

Whether or not Van Buren and certain of his servants could then be prevailed upon to maintain the legends they have established, and continue to provide the house with spectral visitants, is not

known. It is in the orchard that Van Buren has apparently been
seen most. And his butler's apparition has been reported from time
to time under the apple trees. This butler was a hardened toper
who used to sneak off to the orchard to have a quiet snifter, according to Louis C. Jones, Director of the New York State Historical
Association, in his book, *Things That Go Bump in the Night.* One
day, however, after an argument with somebody which apparently
depressed him a bit, he went out to the orchard and hung himself.
Jones also reports that a woman was murdered near the gatehouse.
Within the last generation her lonely, white figure has been seen
moving about in the shadows. Jones says also:

"There were a goodly number of Negroes in the Kinderhook area,
several of whom worked at Lindenwald. Aunt Sarah was a vigorous,
strong-minded martinet who ruled the Van Buren kitchen with an
iron hand and a genius for fine cooking. She ruled it in solitary
glory much of the time, permitting other servants to enter only when
they had her permission, and then they were expected to leave as
soon as possible. Residents have told me that early on Sunday
mornings there still drifts up from the empty kitchen [which, with
its large fireplace, was underneath the dining room] one of the
most delectable smells to be enjoyed in America, the lovely fragrance
of pancakes cooking on a buttered griddle—this at times when the
fires are dead in the stove and the kitchen is empty of all living
persons. I cannot help but wonder if maybe the old cook doesn't
come back and stir a weird batter to drop upon a departed griddle
over a fire that went out long ago. But the pancakes have nothing
to do with Tom, who was the servant of a Mrs. Wagner, a neighbor
of Lindenwald."

At a time between tenants, when the house was temporarily
unoccupied, Mrs. Wagner apparently looked after it. Jones goes
on:

"At last word came that the new owners were soon to appear,
and it seemed advisable to put the house in order. Mrs. Wagner
told Tom to go over to the big house and get the kitchen in shape,
but Tom had known Aunt Sarah all too well, and he was not
sure it was wise to intrude upon one who had been so explicit
about her rights and her domain. After a deal of muttering Tom
went, but his stay was short. He reported: 'I went down into the
cellar and then into the kitchen, but the minute I took up a pan
I heard a sound. As I looked up, down the chimney came Aunt

Sarah. She was covered with soot, but her eyes were blazing, and the ends of her kerchief stood up on her head just like horns. So I said to myself, "Tom, you're getting out of this cellar as fast as you can, and nobody's going to make you go back."' Tom never did go back, and if the pancakes are hers, there must still be times when she rules her kitchen."

We haven't yet touched on nearly all the colorful history of Lindenwald. Van Buren's son John, a gay and carefree bachelor who so delighted in wine, women, and song that he was known locally as "Prince" John, had inherited the house from his father. Rumor has it that a fish pond once graced the front lawn of the large estate, but that Prince John came home so many nights inebriated and fell into the pool that his father was eventually forced to drain it and fill in the hole.

John considered himself to be quite a card sharp, along with his other useless talents, and one night, after his father's death in 1862, he got into a poker game with a few men who were considerably sharper than he. Eventually he was maneuvered into such a tight spot that he wagered on the play of a hand not only his house, Lindenwald, but his mistress, whose name is not recorded. He lost both of them. His opponent was one Leonard Jerome of New York City. After gaining possession of the lovely old home, Jerome brought his family and a retinue of servants up from the city to live there for a period of several years. (It would be interesting if it were possible to know what these servants, who apparently worked in the house long before the day when old Tom was sent over to clean up the kitchen, had to say about Aunt Sarah's ghost.)

Jerome's daughter Jennie was then in her early teens. She was later to grow up, have a successful season in London, marry a nobleman, and bear a son who was—none other than the great Winston Churchill!

Jerome sold the house and it went through several hands, arriving in 1917 into the possession of Dr. Bascom Hugh Birney. His daughter Clementine was given the house at her father's death, and she and her husband, William L. deProsse, and their children, Jean and William Jr., lived there until 1957, when Campbell bought it from them. Jean, her husband, Edward ("Ned") Akers, and their four delightful children, Christopher, Jeffrey, Jennifer, and Jonathan, now live on the Niverville Road near Kinderhook in a house full of antiques that may possibly someday find their way into the Van Buren home if it is turned into a historical monument.

During the time they lived in Lindenwald, all the deProsses heard the ghost (or ghosts) moving about. The doors of the big, old, high-ceilinged house are eight feet high and two inches thick, with large silver-plated knobs. Such doors are hardly likely to open and close themselves because of a slight draft; anyway, drafts are seldom felt there. Yet the sound of doors closing ahead of them as they walked through the house were frequently heard by Mrs. deProsse and members of her family.

Footsteps would precede them up the stairs, all the way to the large attic overhead. Mr. deProsse, whose father was an architect, explains that the sounds were made because the boards were expanding with moisture or shrinking because of drying out. There was a hot-air heating system installed in 1834 which connected seven fireplaces to one chimney, and the deProsses have added another furnace in the basement. His wife and daughter are not satisfied with this explanation, and Mr. deProsse himself wonders how it accounts for a few other incidents they have experienced. One night, for instance, it was very still and windless, and yet he and his wife both heard the shutters of their second-floor bedroom window banging, while at the same time they heard a violin playing in the empty house. Another time Jean was sick in bed upstairs and they heard someone go up to her room. They insisted that she had either been out of bed or that she had received a visitor, although Jean assured them that neither had occurred.

Jean wonders how it explains the nights when she felt someone leaning against her bed. The pressure on the covers beside her was strong enough to wake her up; when she told her mother about it, she learned that this had occurred often to her parent as well. "Of course," Jean says, "these were lovely, friendly ghosts. We weren't frightened of them.

"One night," Jean goes on, "Mother and Father went out for the evening, leaving my brother and me alone in the house with two young people who were living there with us at the time. All of us were in the age range of twelve to fifteen years old. I awoke to hear what I thought was Helen, in the room opposite me, opening and shutting the bureau drawers."

Jean went over to the other girl's room eventually to ask her why she did not go to bed. She found her asleep, and, when awakened, she insisted that she had not been opening and shutting the drawers. In Helen's room the sound was not evident, but back in Jean's room they could both hear the noises resuming—as if coming from Helen's room. "We woke the boys," Jean says, "but everything was quiet after that. Somehow none of us felt like going back to sleep, though, and we all sat up in the kitchen and waited for Mother and Daddy."

When he was unable to hear the noises in the house, Jean's brother Bill was inclined superciliously to attribute them to women's nerves, or old house creakings, until one night when he and his wife Rosalind were sleeping there alone. "Suddenly Roz was awakened by the sound of somebody walking around," Jean says. "She woke Bill and he also heard it." Oddly enough, their golden retriever slept peacefully on the floor beside their bed, never noticing a thing. Usually it is the dogs in ghost houses who give the first warning, but this fellow had no comment on the entire proceedings.

Bill left his wife in the bed, guarded by this sleeping animal, and "tramped all over the house," according to Jean; but he never found a living soul who could be causing the noise. Actually, he never found any other kind of a soul, either. But back in his bedroom again, he and Rosalind were treated to a reprise. Now they panicked, called Jean and Ned to come for them, and returned home with them. The dog went, too, although he had no quarrel with the place he had been.

It was not the haunts that caused the deProsses to sell. They left because the young people had grown up and married and had homes of their own. But Jean Akers and her mother have never lost their interest in Lindenwald, and they are still pondering about who haunts it and why. Mrs. deProsse thinks the ghost is Prince John, reluctant to leave because he had such a good time there.

A man who worked for them once said that the bones of fifteen slaves were buried in the wine cellars underneath, where there are huge wells that were used long ago to cool the wine. Jean does not know where he got his information.

Jean and her brother had always held the theory that there was a secret tunnel under the house, but they were never allowed to dig or to tear out any of the walls in order to find out. Even so, she feels that tunnels would not have explained the phenomena as caused by mere *human* intruders, for if the tunnels existed they were so securely sealed up that nobody could have gotten inside the house by way of them.

All of which brings us right back to the evidence that Aaron Burr may have hidden there. It was acquired in a very intriguing manner. From the time Grandfather Birney bought the house, he had known that there was a sealed room in the attic. The bell tower had been built adjoining it on one side, and on the other two sides were halls. Between, there was a space the size of a room, completely closed off with no means of access. And it had no window on the outside. Once, when Dr. Birney was having the roof of the house re-slated, he had the opportunity to have this secret room examined while the roof was off. He lowered his daughter Marion, Mrs. deProsse's sister, down on a rope through the opening into the sealed room. Inside, she found some old boards and exactly three other objects: a small rocking chair; a tiny carved wooden pig, just about two inches long; and a *calling card* of Aaron Burr's.

So perhaps the servants who formerly worked in the house, and the neighboring farmers, were not exaggerating after all when they said they had seen Burr's ghost wearing a wine-colored coat, with lace at his wrists, wandering about the house and the grounds. If he was hidden there for three years, he no doubt left a memory image there of one kind or another. One who claimed to have seen Burr walk through the orchard said that the wind was blowing a gale at the time, but there was not even a movement of the long lace cuffs—nothing seemed to touch him.

This is typical of the little man, in a way, isn't it? Nothing ever touched him.

CHAPTER EIGHTEEN

NEW ORLEANS REVERIES

THERE IS NOTHING LIKE A REALLY ROMANTIC TALE to break the routine of "authentic" cases—and where would we be more likely to find colorful stories than in New Orleans? That the charm and beauty of this old city should nonetheless be wrapped in the somber garments of hate, fear, and misery is hardly surprising: violence, slavery, pirates, and war were its destiny all the while its beautiful old homes were being constructed.

These houses remember. Practically every courtyard in the French Quarter, hiding behind its wrought-iron gates, claims a hidden body or a tragic crime. Any winding staircase with its graceful curves may climb to a room in which someone was hidden against his will, in which a crying spirit attempts now to make its presence known. Every deserted plantation house in the bayous and swamps, unbelievably, startlingly, disproportionately huge, surrounded by its oak trees dripping with melancholy Spanish moss, has some past horror to endure.

Probing the sinister secrets of the Vieux Carré, we discover the house at 1140 Royal Street, where, in antebellum days, lived the popular Mme. Delphine Lalaurie, whose dinner parties were the toast of society. What dark, depraved twist in her brain made this lovely-looking woman beat and mutilate her slaves? Why did she leave every gathering of friends to torture sadistically the poor human derelicts she kept chained in her attic? It is not surprising that now on dark nights passersby are startled by the screams of a terrified little girl who once leaped to death in the courtyard below, or by the rattling of the chains that bound moaning creatures to their prison walls.

Or, consider the house of Marie Laveau, the greatest of the

Voodoo queens, who was once feared by white and black alike for the occult powers she was alleged to possess. Part Indian, part Negro, part white—she was the last great American witch. Her home at 1020 St. Ann Street was the scene of weird secret rites involving various primitive groups. May not the wild dancing and pagan practices still continue, invisible, but frantic as ever?

General Pierre Gustave Toutant de Beauregard was a man of distinction in his time, and he is a ghost of distinction today. His old home at 1113 Chartres Street, called by some the most beautiful in the Vieux Carré, is now owned by author Frances Parkinson Keyes. In her eighties and unwell, Mrs. Keyes lives here only part of the time. But General Beauregard has never left the place. This great Louisiana Confederate leader resigned as Superintendent of West Point to lead Southern troops in the Civil War. His defeat at the Battle of Shiloh still haunts him, if tradition may be believed.

Built in 1812 by Joseph le Carpentier, the Beauregard House has broad galleries along the front and rear, and granite staircases curving gracefully from each end of its high front gallery. Tall iron gates stand like twin sentinels on guard before the house, protecting the General on his nightly vigils inside. There, at two o'clock in the morning, the vast legions of his followers spring up among the carved rosewood and mahogany, the velvet and brocade, the crystal chandeliers and bronze and marble ornaments of the hall. And then the tattered remnants of an army defeated, the injured and shattered wrecks of a last battalion, fight again the Battle of Shiloh.

Does the hell of the battlefield really appear over and over again at night in this magnificent old mansion? Who can be sure? There are those who claim to have seen it—and they emerge from the house in the morning with pale faces and glassy eyes.

The story that will concern us most has a fairytale quality, for it deals with nothing less engaging than the soft sibilance of sandaled Oriental feet and the swinging of scimitars. Historically there does seem to be some evidence; certainly the Gardette-LePrètre residence has retained its somewhat misleading designation as "The Sultan's House." But the year in which the events allegedly took place varies with the version one reads. In Harnett Kane's column in the New Orleans *Item,* August 8, 1933, and in Helen Pitkin Scherts' *Legends of Louisiana* the dates differ from 1727 to 1792; but the Gardette-LePrètre house was not actually built until 1825.

Constructed by a dentist, Dr. Joseph Coulon Gardette, on the corner of Orleans and Dauphine streets in the Vieux Carré, it was the tallest house in the Quarter, with basements that were farther off the ground and ceilings that were higher than those in any other private house in the city. Four years after its completion the house was sold to M. Jean Baptiste LePrètre, a prominent, respected local merchant and planter. He added to the outside its most distinguishing feature, the galleries whose cast-iron grillwork trim the house with black lace. LePrètre was to own the house until 1878, but when he bought it, he never suspected that it would one day be a seraglio.

Yet, that is just what happened. A vessel of war secretly arrived in the New Orleans harbor one night, and mysterious Turks came and went from it on official business. Finally, a large Oriental potentate of haughty aspect, dressed in regal costume, came ashore and was received with respect by the city officials. New Orleans buzzed. Who was he? Why had he come?

If M. LePrètre was interested in this gossip, his curiosity was quickly satisfied, for it was he who was called into a private conference. He was told that it was his civic duty to cooperate with the efforts to please the honored guest—who was none other than the brother of the Sultan of Turkey.

"Would not M. LePrètre be willing, in order to assist such a person, to allow him the use of his home while in this country?" he was asked.

"You want *my* house?" asked Le Prètre, slightly awed by the honor.

"Indeed, there is no other so stately, so worthy of royalty," the answer came.

And so LePrètre agreed, not knowing that he was taking on what was very definitely a political "hot potato." He was to learn that the man he would lend his home to had stolen his brother's favorite wife, fled with her to Europe, and now had moved on again for safety's sake. He also learned, and with much more chagrin, that the Sultan's brother had also brought his harem with him. He had not only the one little beauty in tow, but four others as well.

LePrètre had to take his wife and children to live at their plantation, and remove from his home all their lovely Creole possessions. Not for Turkish nobility was the tasteful, formal elegance of his furniture. It must all be replaced by carpets from Smyrna and

Persia, soft couches covered with brilliantly embroidered shawls and piled high with colorful cushions, wrought-metal furniture, filigreed fine as honeycomb, carved chests, and golden thuribles of incense. It must have been difficult for LePrètre, particularly as he carried out the little shrine and the holy pictures so beloved by his Catholic family, knowing they would be replaced by the pagan paraphernalia of his heathen guest.

The move was completed and all the trappings of Oriental splendor were finally strewn about. At the very last, incense was burned, candles were lighted, and braziers were heated to warm the rooms; and then the little houris were brought home, carried from the ship rolled in rugs in order to hide them from prying Louisiana eyes.

Soon the five lovely veiled children, whose ages were somewhere between fourteen and sixteen, were as happy here, basking in the admiration and attention of their master, as they would have been anywhere else in the world. Soon the austere house resounded with the patter of their small, red velvet shoes. Daily they were lathered with honey and fine aromatic herbs to bring them beauty and strength. Daily they walked in the courtyard, and their girlish voices were heard by those outside the walls. Their outlandish foreign tongue tantalized the neighborhood men; the rustle of the rare silks of their garments excited the envy and curiosity of the women. But nobody ever saw them. Complete privacy was maintained at all times, the gated front portal was never opened, and the walled garden was constantly patrolled by eunuchs.

One night, several months later, a great storm arose, and an unfamiliar ship with a crescented pennant flying from its mast was seen briefly in the harbor. It was gone the next morning. So also was the storm. But something seemed amiss at the Sultan's house. The gate to the courtyard swung wide on its hinges, and this had never happened before. There were muddy footprints leading in and out of the gate and into the house. And there was no sound anywhere. No titters or happy cries of pleasure, no deep tones of the master could be heard.

Finally alarmed neighbors broke into the house, where they found to their horror several slain servants strewn about. At the foot of the stairway was a tiny, red velvet slipper, and a tall man reached down and picked it up and put it in his pocket. He led the others up the stairs, but all were frightened at what they knew they must see. It was true. In the splendid room above, where the air was heavy with yesterday's incense, mingled with the scent of blood, they discovered them—five young girls, all decapitated.

The brother of the Sultan had also met his death that night, but because of his position he had been carefully buried in the garden. Over the new grave was a marble tablet with the inscription in Arabic: "The justice of heaven is satisfied, and the date tree shall grow on the traitor's tomb." It is said that a tall and stately date tree grew up on that spot, the first of its kind to appear in this country. It was known locally as "the tree of death."

The date tree has long ago perished, and the legends of the old house are fast losing out to modern progress. Yet, as time has gone on, there have been reasons to think that all was not well at the Gardette-LePrètre mansion. For many years it became almost a slum dwelling, as its owners did nothing to keep it in good condition. During its period of worst decay an Italian woman living there washed her clothes and hung them out to dry on the top gallery. One day she fell over the grilled ironwork to the pavement far below, and was killed. She was probably leaning too far backward as she hung the clothes on the line. But the neighbors shook their heads.

"She was pushed," said an Italian woman who lived nearby. By whom? Why? "Never mind," said the woman with a faraway look in her eye.

Holy water was sometimes used to try to lay the ghosts in this house, but it had no effect, for how may blessings of the saints remove the sins of Moslems? But what exorcism could not do, time and modern living have accomplished.

It was long thought that bad luck would come to anyone who sat on the steps leading from the front door down to Dauphine Street. The superstitious feared that the timid little Turkish girls might be peering out at them with eyes of death. But around 1949, when the building housed the New Orleans Academy of Art, the students did not know the superstitions, and did not know they must be afraid. They sat on the steps whenever they wished; and now the timid Turkish girls no longer look out of the house with eyes of death.

It had long been said that the imprint of a tiny shoe was indelibly stained by blood into the floor of the Gardette-LePrètre mansion; but no one who lives there now knows where to look for it.

It was tradition for many years that strange sounds were heard nightly—the thud of a tambour and the piping of flutes as graceful houris danced. Now the noise from nearby nightclubs drowns out any possibility of distinguishing the earthy from the unearthly music. The modern sounds of the night in the Vieux Carré are automobile horns and revving motorcycles. If any frantic footsteps run up and down the stairs, if any frightened screams come from the house, who can distinguish them from late carousers going by, or televisions turned up too loud?

The great iron gates in front of the Dauphine Street steps are never closed now, because the building has been made into apartments. Valued at $143,000, it is managed by twin brothers, Dan and David Nestroy, who have a business interest in the house with their family. It has been divided into nine units, several of which have the unusual apartment feature of being two-storied, as the tall basement has been turned into bedrooms. Many of those who live there are medical students, and the top floor—the scene of the sentimental seraglio—is now a luxurious penthouse belonging to a physician. With this overpowering materialistic influence, the exotic atmosphere of violent long-ago tragedy exists no more.

Yet not everyone has forgotten. Miss Hazel Ogden, a retired practical nurse who has lived just down the block on Orleans Street for thirty-five years, knows. When I asked her about the building on the corner, she said, "Oh, you mean the haunted house!" She added that people often referred to the story of the harem when she first moved into the neighborhood.

"But so many new people have come into the area now," she says. "They just come and go, come and go. Not many oldtimers live in the Quarter any more. So it isn't talked about much."

But, Miss Ogden reflects, people shouldn't be allowed to forget. Such things are important. "That's history," she says. "That's history."

CHAPTER NINETEEN

THE BURNLEY
SCHOOL SPOOK

IN DOING RESEARCH FOR THIS BOOK I have made it a practice never
to visit ghost houses with mediums. If a psychic person has happened to be along, I have noted his impressions; but it has not been
my purpose to attempt to communicate with the alleged entities
who haunt the houses I have visited.

Once, though, I found myself in a haunted school in the company
of four mediums, and it was an experience I'll never forget. This is
what happened.

The Burnley School of Professional Art, at 905 East Pine Street
in Seattle, Washington, had loud creaky footsteps on the stairs and
locked doors that opened in the night for about six years, until they
abated somewhat in the spring of 1965. I made an appointment on
October 4, 1965, with Jess Cauthorn, the owner-director of the
school and one of the Pacific Northwest's best-known watercolorists,
to visit his school and interview several of the students who had
heard unexplained activity in the building. Since I was in Seattle
also to study the manifestations of the medium Keith Milton Rhinehart, we decided to ask him to join us later and see what psychic
impressions he received there.

The Burnley School is on the corner of Broadway and Pine
Street, across from a very old public school now known as Edison
Tech. The Franklin Savings & Loan Association occupies the street-
level offices of the building, and the art school takes up the two
top floors. The structure was originally designed to be a cultural
and art center; and it had studios for ballet and piano and a large
auditorium on the second floor to be used for special events. Its
first official function was a reception for President William Howard
Taft when he visited Seattle to open the Alaska-Yukon-Pacific

Exposition of 1909. For some years a dancing club known as "Entre Nous" used to rent Christiansen's Dance Studio in the auditorium, for student affairs which were the big social events of Broadway High School each season.

There was a period when the auditorium was used as a temporary school gymnasium for the overflow from across the street; but the ceilings were so low that basketball players had to invent trick shots —such as banking the ball off the ceiling. When the dancing teacher complained that the noise was disturbing his classes, wrestling mats were brought and placed against the gym walls to muffle the noise.

In 1946, Edwin Burnley, a well-known Seattle artist, opened art classes there and taught many budding painters, including Jess Cauthorn, who now owns the school. The big gym has been turned into a classroom full of adjustable wooden desks at which students work during the day, and which the ghost apparently resents exceedingly. He makes noises at night as if he were moving the desks around—great scraping and scrunching sounds as if he were trying to drag them out of there. He is better in the audio department than the material or physical, for nothing is ever actually disturbed in the morning—except the people who had to listen to the noises the night before.

Jess Cauthorn told me that he, himself, has heard these manifestations. He had never believed in ghosts until that time. He isn't really sure that he does now, and yet . . .

"I'm a realistic person," Cauthorn said, "but there are some things you just can't ignore—like the sound of desks being moved in an empty room behind locked doors."

Jess thought that perhaps the ghost had been more active in recent years because, "We've had to enlarge the school to accommodate more students. This meant going into strange nooks and crannies, opening up heretofore unused rooms and employing the long-locked-up back stairway in order to get to new classrooms. That's probably what disturbed the ghost, who, apparently had not been too active up until then."

John R. Nelson, a tall young student, illustrated for me the sound the ghost made on the stairs. He went down and clomped up the wide flight leading from the first floor to the third. The steps are very creaky, and each footstep squeaked in its own specific way. There was no possible doubt that the sound was just that—a footstep on a stair. John said that, when he had been working on a big art project and didn't want to stop, he had sometimes painted most of the night. When he was all alone in the building, and knew he was all alone, he would hear, at any moment between eleven o'clock at night and three o'clock in the morning, footsteps mounting those stairs. He would naturally go to see who was arriving, but nobody was there. At least, no physical presence was there.

"I was scared to death at first," said John.

"Can you ever get used to a thing like that?" I asked.

"Not really," he replied. "You just learn not to work here alone at night."

"You wouldn't get me here alone, even without a ghost," I said, being somewhat of a sissy about big, empty places.

"New students don't believe it, of course," John went on. "But after they've been here some of them work late at night and then they hear it. Jennie Miller . . ." and John nodded toward a girl who had just come into the room, "didn't believe it at first. And she even stayed in the building several nights and didn't hear anything. . . ."

"But when I finally did," Jennie interrupted him, "I went bellowing down the hall. I was all alone here and I wanted to run out, but I was scared to go down the stairs."

The students got together and devised tests to catch the haunt. With masking tape they fastened thread across doorways about three feet off the floor. The next day, when they were sure that they had been the last ones out at night and the first ones in in the morning, they found some of the threads broken. On another occasion they stretched the thread across the stairway. Then they turned out the lights and waited upstairs. Some time later, they heard the steps come up both flights; but on examination the thread, which a living being would either have broken or knocked down, was intact.

Lest it be suspected that the noises heard on the stairs were just the normal creakings of old buildings, the students ask how that accounts for the fact that when they hear someone climbing, the creaks are sequential in order from bottom to top.

Cauthorn did not want his students alone there at night if there was any possible danger that a robber could be getting into the place in such a clever way that no one could catch him at it. So he had an insurance investigator check over the building carefully.

When the place was pronounced perfectly safe, with all the locks and doors and windows secure against intruders, Jennie again worked late in her studio.

"While I was concentrating hard on my sketches," she told me, "I heard a bang, and then a creak, and then the sound of somebody walking. Naturally I had all the lights on, and I hurried out into the hall to see who it was. Nobody was there." Later that night she heard a key go into the lock of the front door and the squeaking sound of the door opening. "I rushed out and looked down the stairs," she said, "but the door was not open and not a soul had come in."

Jennie's friend, Ellen Pearce, had a studio on the third floor, and they worked there sometimes at night. The main light switch for that floor is on the inside of a room, and you have to grope your way across in the dark to find it. One night the girls heard a moan behind the door of that room, like a human being in great agony. Wondering who could possibly have gotten in there, and what could be happening, they fumbled their way across to the light switch, almost petrified with fright.

"But can you imagine our state when we got the light on and looked behind the door and no one was there?" asked Ellen.

I could. But I said I'd rather not.

Another student, Robert B. Theriault of Seattle, found a certain small room, used by the students for resting and coffee breaks, to be the most sinister of all. Once, when the lights were on in there, he was standing outside the door, but he knew someone was inside because he heard sounds as if magazine pages were being turned, and other movements. However, when he started to enter the room, the rustling stopped, and there was no one in there.

Henry Bennett is a commercial artist who had an apartment on the third floor while he was a student at the Burnley School around 1959–60. Cauthorn told me, "Hank was responsible for the security of the building at night. But often in the morning I would find the front door, or the fire door, wide open, or at least they would be unlocked when I arrived. Sometimes I really chewed Hank out, but he always insisted he had locked the doors and checked the place over the night before. I didn't know what to think."

Bennett confirmed to me that he always carefully locked the building each night. But the doors were often unlocked the next morning, and sometimes even open. "Many curious things happened while I was living there," he said. "You would swear someone was walking up the stairs or moving furniture in some room, or some unseen person was doing construction work on the building. But when I'd turn on the lights, nobody was ever there." Henry Bennett said that the ghost had not scared him; but he was talking from a distance of five years from the time of the events in which he had been involved.

I was to get close to events within a very short time—for the mediums were gathering. Clyde Beck, a member of the American Society for Psychical Research and an individual who believes in attempting to work with all the equipment of a modern technician, had arrived first, loaded down with movie cameras and tape recorders—none of which were usable when things got interesting. By then we were all in the dark, and he had been unable to secure infrared lights and film. After Clyde, came several of the younger mediums of Rhinehart's church—the Aquarian Foundation. Then came the feature attraction of the evening—Dr. Keith Milton Rhinehart, himself.

Actually an intelligent young man of twenty-nine, Keith was at that time affecting a mustache and goatee and a loud sports jacket— and he looked more like a beatnik guitar player than the pastor of a church. He brought a few more people with him; so it turned out to be altogether a much larger group than we had anticipated.

Since many people know little about mediums except the reputation some of them have for being fraudulent, I think perhaps I should take a moment here to discuss the subject. Extrasensory perception (or ESP) is not uncommon. Those who have a great amount of it are known as mediums, or "sensitives," or "psychics." They may be born with the natural talent in large degree, or they may have some slight ability and decide to improve it by sitting for development in classes at which a trained medium presides.

I have sat in a number of development groups myself, and have begun to exhibit an interesting amount of telepathy—I can sometimes see a picture clearly in my mind of something another person is at that moment thinking. I have on one or two occasions gone into a trancelike state. I was not then completely unconscious, but my mind was "withdrawn" to the extent that I was not consciously instigating the words that were spoken through my mouth, words that purported to come from a deceased entity. Whether or not what I said came from my subconscious, I cannot state. I am only sure that certain information was given through me which I did not consciously know, and had not acquired normally.

Because of my own personal experience with this, I am aware that the material mediums produce may be genuine. I also know the effort, the countless hours sitting in classes, which many sensitives spend in order that their psychic talents may be developed as fully as possible. For this reason I must say definitely and firmly that all mediums are not fraudulent.

Yet I know that, just as there are quack doctors and shyster lawyers, there are phoney mediums. I have seen some who put on such sham acts that it was disgusting; and I have been furious, not only with them but with the gullible public who allowed themselves to be taken in by such trickery.

Keith Rhinehart is a natural-born medium who also spent years improving his native capabilities, beginning when he was in junior high school. When he is in good form, his powers are excellent. I have seen much evidence that, when he is entranced, genuine information has been given through him that he could have no possible normal way of knowing. This is usually referred to as "mental" mediumship. Although extremely adequate as a mental medium, Keith prefers to be known as a "physical" medium—one in whose presence curious physical phenomena occur.

One of his special abilities, it is claimed, is the production of "apports"—objects that are said to have been dematerialized from somewhere else on earth and then rematerialized inside the seance room. If the room has been thoroughly searched beforehand, the possibility of trap doors and secret compartments and false arms and bottoms to chairs, etc., eliminated, and the medium has been stripped and examined by a doctor, and *then* apports appear during the seance—it is hard not to consider their appearance as a supernormal manifestation. In the history of psychical research there is evidence for the appearance of apports, under conditions that have been so controlled as to give no opportunity for fraud.

I have seen apports appear in a lighted room under what I considered to be controlled conditions; but still I am reluctant to declare firmly once and for all that the phenomena were genuine. Many investigators much more highly trained than I have also hesitated to commit themselves. This is because there are some mediums who are so adept at prestidigitation that it is difficult for anyone ever to guarantee absolutely that he might not have in some way been hoodwinked.

I am going into this in such detail because of the events which followed at the Burnley School. I want it understood that I do not point an accusation of fraud at anybody for what occurred on the evening I am about to describe. And yet there is no possible way for me to be certain that there was not at least some lighthearted trickery involved. Then again, maybe there wasn't. After all, we were in a building with a reputation for being haunted.

The members of Keith's organization who came with him to the Burnley School that night had trained themselves very carefully, sitting hour after hour in dark rooms letting their natural medium-istic talents develop. I felt, and still feel, that they are sincere workers at their trade. In this group were Judith Crane, a very pretty, well-educated young woman who has gained considerable prominence as a medium, and her fiancé, Donald Ballard, whom she has since married. Don is not a medium and is only a follower of psychic interests insofar as they affect Judy. I can't help but believe that Don would have been furious if he had observed in Judy or her associates anything he thought was in any way dis-honest—yet he was with the Aquarian Foundation members all the time that evening. The two other Aquarians present were Kenneth Bower and Helen Lester. The rest of the crowd that began to tour the haunted school included Jess Cauthorn, his students John Nelson and Jennie Miller, Clyde Beck, and me.

As we moved through the building I took notes on the impres-sions each sensitive expressed. Some were interesting in the light of the history of the school: It was sensed that there had been dancing and basketball in the big auditorium and that there had been exercise mats there at one time. But all this had been published in various newspaper accounts of the haunting which had appeared over the years, one as recent as June 1965, so the mediums could be given no special credit for their successes even if they were genuine "hits." There is always the chance that they may have read the articles.

Several persons stated that a young man had been killed in or near the building long ago, and that he still hangs around and wants to dance and play basketball and have fun as he used to. (Un-fortunately for the veracity of the tale, checks with the police since then have revealed no record of a killing in or near the school. An

Associated Press reporter made a serious effort to track down verification of a murder, but with no results.)

We first decided to try to hold a seance in an area of the basement that had an unpaved dirt floor and old boards and boxes stacked in the corners. There we turned off the lights and sat at first with only one small candle. After a moment, we put that out and sat in the dank dark. Fortunately for my peace of mind, after later developments, some of the girls decided that there might be rats down there, and so we adjourned upstairs. At that time, none of us was in the least afraid of the ghost.

We finally chose a small room on the second floor, just large enough to hold the ten of us, and we put opaque screens over the windows and turned out all the lights. Just enough glow came in around the edge of the screens from the streetlight outside so that we could dimly see those closest to us. Keith and I sat on a short couch, and the others milled about in the dark for a while.

In order to learn if there might be any spirit about who wanted to make an effort to communicate, all those in the room except Keith and me put their fingers on the top of a tall stool. Almost at once it began to move around, so fast that they kept up with it only with difficulty. The stool banged itself with great force against the floor and the wall. It was asked to answer questions in code, with one rap for "Yes" and two for "No"; and it did give some answers this way to a few questions. But whatever was propelling the stool had no interest in such attempts to talk. It preferred to show off its force by banging itself senselessly against the wall.

Keith and I got monstrously bored watching this—it is very routine in mediumistic circles. Catching me yawning, he asked if we should call it all off and go home.

"In a few minutes," I said, "if nothing else happens."

Soon the game with the stool palled on the participants, and they all settled down quietly, pulling their chairs into a circle facing Keith and me. After a few moments of extreme silence, when the full impact of the darkness crept over us, I glanced toward Keith—and suddenly realized that he was staring at me fixedly with the most malevolent expression I have ever had directed my way. He kept it up, not moving, for at least three minutes. The way he looked, with his dark hair, glittering eyes, mustache, and goatee, one could almost suspect that the devil himself had become incarnate in our midst. Not being quite unsophisticated enough to believe *that*, I decided instead that the medium must have been taken over into trance, and prepared myself for a discussion with some spirit entity who was obviously "earthbound" and must be convinced that he should stop haunting this school. I began racking my brain for suitable phrases from those who had published their experiences involving other such delicate situations.

"Who are you?" erupted suddenly and loudly from the medium. I jumped a foot and a half into the air and started to shake. "We're here to help you," I quavered. Then I began to explain to him that he had passed through the experience called death and that he must adjust himself to that fact and go away and stop bothering the people at this school—that there were helpful spirits around him who would give him advice and assistance if he would but listen to them. . . .

"I'm not dead," he shrieked, interrupting me. Then he lunged at me, waving his arms, and shouted, "Get out! Get out, all of you!" And no matter how much I talked to him he kept repeating this refrain with the appropriate motions. It was coming to my attention that the techniques that may have worked for those glib writers who had calmed obstreperous entities with a few well-chosen words were not likely to be so successful in my case. I started on a new tack.

"Did you know it is the year 1965?" I asked.

Keith almost leaped out of his seat. "No, no," he cried. Then apparently taking a second to estimate, he added, "That would make me sixty years old. I'm not old. I'm young!" Yet, as if the idea of his death were beginning to penetrate after all, he began to mutter about blood and a knife. "Blood all over everything," he said, and then such things as: "He got me in the back. I just wanted to stay here and play games and dance but John did me in. He did it; blood, blood, it spurted! The knife dripped blood! John did it. He always hated me." Then, as if taking me for his false friend John he leaned toward me once again, with a look of utter viciousness, and shouted into my face, "Get out, all of you. Go away and leave me alone."

As this dialogue is now written, from notes made the day after the episode, I am appalled by how silly it all was. Even as I sat there participating in this drama, the realization was very present that it was overplayed and amateurish. In retrospect the whole evening seems a trivial travesty of a bad movie or a television turkey.

But while the events were going on and I was participating in them, it was rather necessary to take them at face value, which was not in the least comfortable when the entranced medium kept jumping my way threateningly from time to time. Finally, he lunged and waved his arms in my direction just once too often and I got up and moved over to a bench just opposite the couch. The Thing, whoever it was, by then was muttering irresponsibly to himself, and I saw him glance down at my expensive camera which was on the floor beside where my feet had been. Lest he be inspired to break it, I reached over and picked it up.

As I did so, the maniacal look on Keith's face made me think, "Oh, if I could just get a picture of this for the book." I began to sight the camera at him. Fortunately, I did not have time to flash the bulb—for if it is true, as I have since learned that all spiritualists believe, that any flash of light or sudden shock might kill an entranced medium, it might have been I instead of a ghost who was the villain of this piece.

When the camera went up to my eye, Keith cried, "What are you doing?" and made a leap for me.

I shouted, "Don't you touch me!" and kicked him. It was just a little kick—and it barely connected with his leg; but he plummeted to the floor as if I had landed a rock on his skull. I didn't do anything then for a minute but sit and quiver. Then I began to worry for fear the medium was badly injured, because he was lying there prone, breathing as if each gasp might be his last. I had not more than touched him, but it was evidently enough to have caused the entity to lose his hold.

All of us sat with eyes glued on him, to see if he would come out of it; finally, we heaved sighs of relief as we heard the deep sonorous tones of the medium's special "spirit guide," who acts as his "control" and takes care of him, saying through him, "This is Dr. Robert John Kensington, and we have things in hand." Keith, still entranced, but now by his proper control, got up and sat back on the couch, Dr. Kensington apologizing all the while for having allowed him to be taken over by such an irresponsible entity. He said that he had not realized that the spirit was actually insane until he had gotten into Keith's body; and that the number of mediums present acted as a battery that gave the entity more power.

Keith then came out of his trance, asked for a drink of water, and sat holding his head, complaining of a violent headache. He asked what had happened, and somebody began to tell him. I was doing a lot of thinking, very negatively. If this had all been an act, it was such an overdone performance that it was hardly worthy of Keith's histrionic ability. . . . yet if it had not been put on—Good Heavens! I'd been in real danger! I turned and said, perhaps a bit sarcastically: "How did it happen, may I ask, that all of you sat there so calmly while I was being attacked by a maniac?"

The Aquarian Foundation members told me that they knew that touching the medium when he was in such a state would have injured him.

"But what if I had been injured?"

"You didn't have a thing to worry about," they assured me. "We were surrounding everyone with protective thoughts, so everything was completely under control." Under control? I almost had a camera wrapped around my head!

Keith had nearly been clobbered, too, Jess Cauthorn told me later. When we had a long retrospective chat about the evening's experiences he said that he and John Nelson had been sitting on the edges of their chairs, signaling each other, and ready to spring if the medium got one inch closer to me. They had been considering the entire thing to be a clumsy hoax; but they wondered why, if it was a hoax, Keith had not known he was going too far and would be in danger from them if he got the least bit rough. This was part of the whole big mystery. If he was putting on an act, why did he not realize the possibility of being physically restrained by those two men so much larger than he? There were many mysteries about this evening that have never been resolved; and this was one of them. Yet the biggest mystery of all occurred after we left the seance room. It put a slightly different light on the whole performance. But it did not solve anything. It only made the confusion worse.

Rather depressed by the episode that had just taken place, I had gathered my nerve, my wits, and my camera and walked out of the seance room to try to get another picture or two of the school building. I was accompanied by Keith and Clyde Beck. The others remained in the room and then spread out, eventually going downstairs. The three of us walked back down the hall and into the auditorium, around a corner and about fifty feet from the seance room. After discussing the possibility of getting a photo of the large room, and deciding it would be useless to try with my equipment, I started to walk back up the hall. Hearing a funny sound from Keith, I turned to look at him. His eyes were getting that glassy, glittery look again, and he began to mumble, "I told you there was something I could do you couldn't" and other phrases that weren't particularly intelligible. He approached me menacingly.

"It's got him again," I shrieked, rushing up the hall away from him. "Clyde, *do* something!" Clyde did something; he watched to see what was going to happen next. I moved on as quickly as possible, hollering to the people downstairs. Aquarians came bounding up, and as they did the medium began to speak once more in the deep tones of his control. "This is Dr. Robert John Kensington," he said. "The entity got back in once again because there was something he insisted on saying. Will you please call the owner of the building?"

Jess Cauthorn was just arriving up the stairs on a run, and he said breathlessly, "I'm here."

"Do you recall if there was a rock about the size of a brick in that room where the seance was held?" Dr. Kensington asked.

"No, I don't think so," answered Jess. "I'm almost sure there was not."

"Well, the entity was trying to say that he had the power to bring apports," the voice went on. "Now if you will go into the seance room you will find a rock there close to where Miss Smith was sitting."

We all rushed into the room, and sure enough, right where my feet had been when I sat on the end of the bench, there was now a smooth, oval rock as large as a brick. It could not have been there when my feet were cringing in that spot a few minutes before.

The next day, at my suggestion, students went into the basement of the school building and reported that they found a hole the exact size, into which the rock fit neatly. It was in an area of the dirt where there were a few other similar stones scattered about. They immediately decided that this was the proof they needed that the whole thing had been a hoax. But it really wasn't necessarily that convincing. Even if the rock had come from there, this would not prove it wasn't an apport, because an apport has to come from somewhere; and the spirit would not in that brief interval have gone wandering afar to dig one up. He was said to be haunting *this* place. If he had decided he wanted a rock to heave at me, would he have thought of looking anywhere else for it?

As can be imagined, we all did a great deal of arguing and conjecturing for days afterward. All except Keith Milton Rhinehart, who went home with a terrible headache and was said to have been confined to his bed. As we thought about the apport and tried to explain it, we realized that the medium, being a rather slight man, could not possibly have hidden so large a rock on his person in order to bring it up from the basement without being observed. If one of the women members of the Aquarian Foundation had managed to secrete it somewhere (in some oversize handbag?) how did Keith, down the hall with me, know about it?

The only answer, except one really dealing with ghosts and apports and other supernormal things, is that the whole event was an extravaganza put on by the entire group of mediums in collaboration, to show the visiting author a good time and give her something to write about. But Keith and all the others knew that I was prepared to write scathingly about them if I discovered them in anything fraudulent, or even in anything particularly suspicious looking. They were aware, moreover, that they had much more at stake than a haunted school, for I was in Seattle investigating whether or not the phenomena of all Keith's services and seances were genuine; and I had a magazine contact that they knew was eager for the story. Why, under those circumstances, would they play stupid games with me? Why also would Keith have run the risk of being injured when he leaped at me, knowing full well that the non-Aquarians in the group would certainly have defended me?

Although my experience at the Burnley School was effective enough to scare me temporarily out of my wits, it could not have been permanently convincing. Of all the questions raised by this incident, the biggest that remains it this: If the Aquarians *had* decided to put on an act, why wasn't it a *better* act? These were intelligent adults, not children; they couldn't have been stupid enough to have produced such an overblown, overacted melodrama and expected it to be believed.

But an old, earthbound spirit so dumb as to hang around a school for sixty years without knowing it was time to graduate—he might have acted just the way he did that night. After all, we *were*

in a building in which a great many genuinely unexplainable manifestations had already occurred.

I came out of this whole adventure with only one conclusion:
You'd better keep your cool if you're going with an old school
ghoul.

CHAPTER TWENTY

MIAMI'S PERTINACIOUS POLTERGEIST

IT ISN'T OFTEN that a spook sleuth in the midst of writing a book about ghosts is lucky enough to have a genuine poltergeist case fall right into her lap. But this happened to me when I was in Miami, Florida, in January 1967, at the time that crockery began to crash at Tropication Arts, Incorporated, 117 N.E. 54th Street. I am therefore able to present a day-by-day report of what can be said at the outset, with reliable official substantiation, to be one of the most interesting poltergeist cases in American history. Its manifestations, it is true, were limited to throwing and breaking things in one warehouse, but they often occurred in the presence of as many as fifteen people at a time, tantalizing everyone from policemen to preachers, and even parapsychologists.

On Thursday afternoon, January 12, I was being interviewed by Bill Smith on radio station WKAT in Miami. The subject under discussion was the work I was currently doing on this book. As we talked, the telephone button began to flicker frantically, and I was soon conversing with Bea Rambisz, who said she was an artist for a firm that sold wholesale novelties and souvenirs. She told me that glass beer mugs were flying off the shelves there, and other things were dashing about when nobody was anywhere near enough to throw them. She said these curious events had increased in intensity as the day progressed, and were now occurring so frequently that the people working there were becoming alarmed. What, she asked, did I recommend that they do to stop this annoyance?

Stop it? It sounded as if a poltergeist had gone berserk among their belongings, and there was nothing I wanted to see more than a genuine poltergeist in action.

"Just hang on and keep calm until I can get out there and observe it," I told her. And they did. Or rather, it hung on to them.

I wasn't too sure that this was any more than the typical tribulations of those who so often telephone to radio talk programs about haunts which turn out to be hallucinatory; so it wasn't until 11:30 the next morning, Friday the 13th, that I got around to going to Tropication Arts. Once I got there, I seldom left the establishment for the next twenty-four days, except when I was run out at closing time. Before it was all over I had notes on approximately three hundred incidents, and I had acquired statements from scientists, magicians, newspaper and television people, and dozens of others, many of whom were willing to testify that they saw things in motion or heard objects clatter to the floor at a time when they knew the position of every person in the room and were sure no one could possibly be throwing things. They also stated that they had examined the area of the action carefully to make sure that there was no device of any kind which might have propelled the object into space.

Perhaps it would be best to tell some of my own experiences first. Then they can be corroborated by the reports I heard from others.

"I don't believe it, but it's really happening. I saw it with my own eyes," is the first statement I heard as I identified myself to Ruth May, the pretty woman who met me at the door of Tropication Arts. She kept repeating this over and over again as she led me across the musty, cluttered room full of work tables at which she and two other artists painted palm trees and other Florida symbols on salt and pepper shakers, plastic purses, manicure kits, and the usual souvenir novelties. Mrs. May took me into an office and introduced me to Alvin Laubheim, the manager.

"I don't believe in ghosts," was Laubheim's greeting to me. "But something we can't see is making a shambles of our warehouse." While we were pocketed in his small office discussing the peculiar nature of the happenings, there was a thud from another room. Everyone, with me in tow, rushed into the warehouse at the back of the building where we found two men and a girl pointing excitedly to a box lying on its side in an aisle between two tiers of shelves. From it were spilling a number of little plastic pencil sharpeners shaped like TV sets.

"It just fell, all by itself!" the girl said.

I'd read about poltergeists for years and wished to see one operate, but I wasn't going to be railroaded into instant enthusiasm about something anyone could have knocked off a shelf. Still, I got out my notebook and started to ask each person in the room where he had been standing, what he had been doing, etc. They all corroborated each other's statements that nobody had been near when the incident occurred. All those who gathered around me sounded the same refrain as they told me about the things they had experienced, "I don't believe it, but I saw it happen!"

As time went on and I was with them day after day, I came to like the various employees of this firm: the artists, Ruth May, Bea Rambisz, and Patricia Wolfe; Iris Rolden, the tiny eighteen-year-old Cuban girl who sat at the desk in the front of the stockroom and pasted or stamped "Florida" on each object; Rolando Santovenia, the bookkeeper, who remained in his front cubicle, stoically refraining from excitement over any of the poltergeist activity; and those most involved in it—the shipping clerks, Julio Vasquez, a nineteen-year-old Cuban boy, and Curt Hagemeyer, an older man who had just begun to work there the previous Monday.

My first reaction was that the warehouse was a very disorganized place. A vast amount of useless milling about seemed to be going on, as Julio and Curt wandered aimlessly up and down the aisles between the shelves in the middle of this warehouse room. It turned out that there was a reason for this.

Al Laubheim, the large, gregarious, easygoing man who manages the flourishing twenty-one-year-old business that sells wholesale novelty and souvenir items to dime stores, gift shops, and drug stores, is also part owner. His partner, Glen Lewis, a more quiet type, has a penchant for organization—or rather, reorganization. Lewis had begun rearranging the boxes and cartons in which the souvenirs are stored in an attempt to place the shelves in systematic order. He was obviously right in attempting to get some order there; but, unfortunately his efforts to improve the place had started at just about the same time that the poltergeist had thrown everything and everybody into an uproar. So not only were the shipping clerks unnerved, they were also unsettled in their ways. The bemused expressions on Julio's and Curt's faces as they wandered up and down the aisles were not entirely due to the strange phenomena going on there. To fill their orders they were searching for supplies, which to them had been misplaced, and at the same time they were stepping over boxes and bottles that had been maliciously broken on the floor by the invisible prankster in their midst. Laubheim and Glen Lewis were tearing their hair over the damage being done to the property. All the girls were wasting time gabbing about the poltergeist instead of working. And on top of everything else, no one was sure whether or not their unseen antagonist might decide at any moment to break a bottle over someone's head or unleash his fury in some other dangerous manner.

Iris Rolden told me, "Just a little while ago I was talking to Julio when I saw a big cardboard carton on top of a shelf start to move by itself. It fell down. I ran away screaming and crying."

Julio, whose heart pounded wildly every time something crashed, said that this box, which he had also seen, had actually seemed to fly across the space between the tiers of shelves. It lit momentarily on the top of the opposite tier, and then tumbled to the floor. I had Julio take the carton back to a scale and weigh it. It hit the eight-pound mark, and that's a relatively heavy thing to go bounding about by itself.

Ruth May told me that, for about a month before, an occasional beer mug would break. "I thought the boys in the back room were playing games," she said. Al Laubheim confirmed this, saying that he had ordered the boys to be more careful, and had paid no attention to them when they insisted they had not been breaking things. Then, the day before, the activity had suddenly gotten much worse.

Just a short while before I had arrived, Ruth had been sitting at the desk where Iris usually works, at the south end of the warehouse. Out of the corner of her eye she saw something move and ran toward it as it fell. She found that it consisted of four pasteboard boxes tied together, which contained inflatable beach balls. I weighed these also, and they totaled nine pounds. Still I remained skeptical. I had to observe one of these moving objects myself. This I did, almost immediately, for a noise in the aisle back of me made me turn in time to see a box land on the floor, spilling out small plastic fans. No one was anywhere near the shelf from which the box had dropped, but who could be sure that somebody at the other end of the tier might not have thrown it and then jumped quickly aside? The shelf on which it had been stored with other similar boxes of fans was smooth and dry. I could see nothing there to account for the activity.

The warehouse room is thirty by fifty feet, running north and south. It had floor-to-ceiling shelves along the east wall, desks or work tables across the front and back, and three tiers of shelves in the middle of the room. I have designated the aisle between the wall shelves and the first tier as One, and the aisle along the west wall as Four. Aisles Two and Three are, of course, on each side of the middle-shelf tier.

After lunch I placed myself at an observation point at the north end of the room in Aisle One, next to a work table, where I could watch all the people puttering around in the room: Glen Lewis, busily rearranging boxes, and Julio and Curt trying to find them again. In quick succession, the following occurred:

At 1:50 P.M., when all three of the men were close to me and directly within my line of vision, we heard something fall in Aisle Four near the west wall. It proved to be a box of rubber daggers and sheaths. While the four of us—the only people in the room—were gathered around the daggers, examining them and the shelf from which they fell, there was a crash over in the first aisle, some twenty-five feet away. There we found a china sailfish ashtray smashed to bits. By the time I had settled back into my chair and begun to make notes of these incidents, a box containing imitation leather coin purses fell into Aisle Four. Moments later, as Julio, intent on cleaning up the remains of the ashtray, walked up Aisle One with a broom in one hand and a dustpan in the other, a shot glass fell behind him. He was within a foot of me when the glass jigger hit the cement floor with a loud retort, yet it wasn't even so much as nicked.

When I had to leave soon afterward, it was with the conviction that something unusual was definitely afoot at Tropication Arts. This was hardly an odd assumption, under the circumstances. Yet I argued with myself constantly as soon as I had left the shop, certain that there was some clue I had overlooked. Perhaps there was some kind of trigger I didn't know about, like a rubber band which would snap back and remain unseen on the shelf after causing a box to fall. Or dry ice against which a dish could have been tilted until the ice melted and threw the dish off balance and onto the floor. I even talked myself into thinking that perhaps my powers of observation were not as sharp as I thought—perhaps someone had rigged a shelf with a propulsive agent without me or anyone else there noticing it. I was a clever detective at night at home.

But the next day, back on my self-appointed job, I was as befuddled as all the rest.

Knowing that I was not sufficiently qualified by training or experience to give this curious affair a proper scientific investigation, I had put in a long-distance call the first night to my friend W. G. Roll, the project director of the Psychical Research Foundation of Durham, North Carolina, with whom I have worked before. Unfortunately, there had been a death in his family, and so I was on my own for a week before Bill Roll could arrive. By then, Tropication Arts was a madhouse. Reporters, cameramen, and radio people swarmed everywhere. The Miami *Herald* and the *News* ran our pictures on their front pages. United Press International called from New York, and Al put me on to tell them that I really thought there was some genuine poltergeist phenomena going on. The Associated Press representative arrived in person, however, and saw enough bounding bric-a-brac to convince himself that this was really something spectacular.

The press had learned of the story as an aftermath to Saturday's activities. On that day Al Laubheim had really begun to fear that someone might be hurt in the warehouse, and so he did what any other normal red-blooded American male would do in a similar circumstance—he summoned the police. Patrolman William Killin responded to the call and was talking to Al in the office when he heard his first smashup from the stockroom. He then cased the room thoroughly, carefully examining everything, pushing boxes back on shelves in the event that they had been falling off under their own momentum, and looking for evidence of fraud or trickery. As Killin turned his back on Aisle Four momentarily, a glass shattered behind him. Whirling around, Killin ascertained that no one in the room was in any position to have instigated the action. He scrutinized the remains of the glass and found nothing in them or on the shelves above that might have caused the damage. Killin was cautiously curious, but by the time four other objects sailed from their home bases, he was, as I had been, "hooked" on the idea that there was no explanation for what he had observed. So he did what any other normal red-blooded American police officer would have done—he telephoned for his superior.

"You'd better come over here, sir," he told Sergeant William McLaughlin. "There's something mighty strange going on."

"Well, can't you save me a trip and tell me about it on the phone?" asked McLaughlin.

"No, sir, I'm afraid I can't," answered Killin.

As we all soon learned around there, our poltergeist was sneaky and tricky and seemed to know what it was doing. When we were looking in one place for evidence, it operated in another spot quite far away. When the most skeptical persons were present, it frequently remained absolutely silent—with a few major exceptions that I will relate later. So, although Patrolmen David J. Sackett and Ronald Morse, who accompanied McLaughlin, saw a few incidents which triggered their interest, Sgt. McLaughlin was never in a position to be sure that someone might not have thrown the few things that crashed while he was there. He telephoned me later on Saturday afternoon, at Al's suggestion, to inquire about poltergeists and their habits, and I told him they are mysterious phenomena that have occurred throughout the world down through the ages, and that there is no normal explanation for their feats. McLaughlin reserved his judgment. He also moved Officer Killin to Point Control so that he would not have to make any more calls on the haunted warehouse. Even so, Killin acquired the nickname "Caspar the Friendly Ghost" from his mates, and was greeted with an occasional ghoulish moan as he came on duty. But Killin hasn't changed any of his opinions except, as we all have, to doubt his own powers of observation from time to time as he remembers the experience.

During these hectic days, Sackett and Morse had checked all the neighboring firms, and canvassed all the homes and businesses in the entire block to learn if anyone else was undergoing similar disturbances. They were not. Sackett, along with others as time went on, verified that sonic booms were not the cause, nor gas accumulations, nor underground water currents, nor any other known natural sources or resources that might conceivably be involved. A geiger counter was even introduced into the warehouse at one time, with no noticeable reactions. We all shook the shelves often, and proved to ourselves that objects could not be shaken off them, nor could they be blown off by the large and powerful electric fan, and they could hardly even by nudged off by a careless elbow.

Officer Sackett, together with magician Howard Brooks, has one of the best-observed incidents in this case to report. Brooks, a

professional magician for some thirty-five years, has been a friend
of Al Laubheim's for even longer—they went to camp together when
they were boys; but their friendship nearly broke up over the
poltergeist. When Al had begun to talk about the crazy things
going on in his business, Brooks taunted him unmercifully.

"What kind of gullible fool are you?" he asked. "You obviously
have an employee who is playing tricks. I can make things crash
from shelves, too, when nobody is near them. Just a little piece of
string and some spirit gum will do it easily. Or some dry ice. Any
magician can do this."

These aren't the kindest words in the world to take from a friend,
especially when you are convinced that the friend doesn't know
what he is talking about. Al was justifiably edgy when Brooks
visited him on Saturday to expose the fraud. In so doing, the
magician proposed to play a bit of a prank himself. "Spook!
Spook!" he shrieked delightedly as everyone came running when
he had surreptitiously tossed a plate on the floor and broken it.
Yet nobody was impressed when he showed them how easily he
had fooled them. They'd seen better acts than his a dozen times
a day by then.

Still, Brooks was intrigued enough by the mystery to return on
Monday, January 16, to continue his investigation. He hadn't yet
caught on to just how the culprit, who he was sure existed, was
perpetrating his crimes. Officer D. J. Sackett was also there that
day. His day off, he had brought in his wife so that she, too,
could see some of the oddities that he had witnessed.

While Howard Brooks, still in his truculent mood, was standing
at the north end of the warehouse, looking south toward the three
rows of shelves in the center of the room, Sackett and his wife
happened to be standing at the south end of Aisle Three and looking toward the west. At that moment two boxes fell together from
the top shelf into Aisle Four. Although nobody saw them actually
leave the shelf, both Sackett and his wife and Brooks observed them
in flight and watched them land neatly on the floor, one on top
of the other as they had fallen. The only other people anywhere
near, Julio and Curt, were in completely opposite directions from
the area, attending to their own business.

When Brooks and Sackett rushed to the shelf there was no
evidence of foreign substances of any kind which could have caused
the boxes to move, without themselves remaining on the shelf after-

ward. No string and spirit gum, no dry ice, nothing small enough to be invisible could have moved objects so large. The two boxes, which, as Sackett noted, "remained curiously together as they fell," weighed four pounds.

"Any paraphernalia," says Brooks, "which would move that weight would have to have been visible when we arrived there immediately afterward." Officer Sackett agrees. He knows that nobody was near enough to that shelf to move those boxes, and he knows that boxes don't propel themselves from shelves alone—or do they?

Officer Sackett, Brooks, and I tried a little experiment with an empty Coca Cola bottle one day. Expecting the cooperation of the poltergeist, we carefully placed the bottle far back on the second shelf of Tier Three and then moved away from it—but not far enough away so that anyone could have reached the shelf without our observing his every act. No one even approached; but within brief minutes, as soon as our attention was momentarily distracted somewhere else, the bottle was dashed to the floor.

A curious commentary about the capricious critter we call "noisy ghost" is that anywhere it manifests it likes to work without supervision. Ours was willing to dash any dishes and crash any crockery that we planted for its attention—it loved the crackling, splintering, spine-chilling crunch they made as they hit the cement—but it would never cooperate as long as the area was watched. One afternoon the CBS television people trained their lights and cameras on Aisle Four for several hours. I told them nothing would happen, and nothing did. But as soon as the cameras were folded and the lights tucked away, beer mugs banged with their usual aplomb.

Sometimes our haunt might shoot a little shot glass into Aisle Three or scatter some address books in Aisle Two so that we would all run there. Then, when we were thoroughly diverted, a large ashtray would suddenly break at the opposite end of Aisle One, or a carton of beer mugs would carom across the room and crash in Aisle Four. True, one seldom saw them flying; but they often moved from a place where they had been observed earlier, to come to an undignified end in a distant spot.

Those who could lay genuine claim to having observed objects in flight were the prima donnas of the warehouse crowd. Among them was a friend of Al's who insisted she had seen a beer mug *leave* the shelf and move straight out parallel with the floor, then change direction abruptly and fall to its finish. Reverend Richard A. Seymour, a Baptist minister, saw a box of plastic pencil sharpeners while it was in motion. Ruth May saw an Orange Crush bottle as it was falling. It landed on its neck and the neck broke off, then the rest of the bottle bounced three times on its side. I once heard a bump and turned in time to see a box plummeting to the floor and spilling out a number of plastic binoculars.

One day Howard Brooks and an attractive young woman named Brenda Gibson were standing near the desk at the front of Tier One, and I was with UPI photographer Dave Haylock at the opposite end of the tier when a plastic tumbler crashed in Aisle One. Dave and I reached the spot in time to see the glass still bouncing and quivering, and he got a picture of it. Then we learned that Howard and Brenda had actually seen it in flight. "The glass wasn't flying, and it wasn't falling directly to the floor, but it rather fell at an angle," Brooks said. Always critical, even of his own observation, Brooks stated that he could not be absolutely positive that someone might not have thrown the glass from the doorway between the warehouse and the front office. As we were puzzling about the possibility of this and that, a voice from the back door said, "I saw it, too."

The back of the warehouse has huge sliding doors that are left open during the day, with an iron grating across them to protect the property. Now, as it had turned out, the barriers were most useful for restraining crowds of noisy, jostling gapers. The large plate glass windows in front of the building had to be covered on the inside with newspapers to keep people from breaking them in, because they were pushing so hard trying to see the ghost. Someone standing at the back door had now called out to us. It proved to be Airman Second Class Robert Gugino, home on leave from Mather Air Force Base, California. Robert testified that he had happened to be looking in the direction of that aisle when he saw something in motion, rising into the air and coming down. He said he was not sure where it had started from, but he thought it must have come from the second shelf of the tier against the east wall.

Now, what in the world would make things fly like this in a simple, somewhat disorganized, quite cluttered, but still commonplace warehouse? What made the Bell Witch? What caused the uproar in the House of Flying Objects in Seaford, Long Island, in 1958? What causes any poltergeist activity? Nobody knows. There are theories, but no definitive statement has ever been spoken, nor is one likely to be given any time soon. Parapsychologists are the ones who will ultimately publish the words that explain the phenomena, especially if they have many more instances to investigate as rewarding as the Miami one.

W. G. Roll was enough impressed with this case that he called in a cohort—Dr. J. Gaither Pratt, with whom he had investigated the Herrmann's poltergeist in Seaford, Long Island. Dr. Pratt was second in command to Dr. J. B. Rhine at the Parapsychology Laboratory when it was at Duke University. Now he is in the Medical Department of the University of Virginia.

In the presence of both Roll and Pratt our contentious invisible busybody acted up just as it always had. Both of them were in the room on various occasions when articles fell. Several instances were so well-controlled that Bill and Gaither were able to know where everyone in the room was standing at the time, and in one or two events all were under direct observation at the moment of impact.

Scientists are not likely to make formal utterances to the effect that they have proved anything, or that they have observed anything conclusive. But here, W. G. Roll says, "I found no evidence that the phenomena were caused by normal means." (He means that he found no indications of trickery or fraud.) And Gaither Pratt states, "I consider the case worthy of careful study and reporting in the scientific literature of parapsychology." From them, that's high acclaim.

Bill Roll isolated us as much as possible from the media people, and it never even got in the papers that Pratt had arrived. The researchers couldn't keep everyone in the room under observance when there were dozens in there milling about, as there had been for so long. We even had to protect ourselves from all those many visitors who came with the good intention of ridding the place of its evil spirits by magic spells, incantations, exorcisms, or what have you. We quite frankly did not want to be rid of it, because we were having one of those once-in-a-lifetime opportunities to observe the activities of a poltergeist under as nearly as possible controlled conditions.

In all poltergeist investigations, some one individual is almost always discovered around whom the activity seems to center. (Poltergeists, whatever they are, haunt people instead of houses.) Parapsychologists declare, therefore, that some psychokinetic force from that individual is used by him unconsciously to produce the manifestations. Spiritualists, of course, say a deceased entity is mysteriously throwing things—and that he gets the power for his actions from the psychic force that is pent up in one particular living individual. In the Miami poltergeist case there had never been any indication that someone wanted to communicate from the spirit world, and certainly there had been no talking, rapping, production of ghostly figures, or any of the other shenanigans indulged in by the Bell Witch. And yet, as I have suggested, our poltergeist somehow seemed to know when people weren't paying attention—almost like a petulant child.

Glen maintained facetiously that it was Al's pet monkey, Lisa. The tiny squirrel monkey that had disappeared and presumably died several months before had thrown anything she could get her hands on during her life. In fact, her last living act toward Al was to squash an egg on his head. In the warehouse, Al or Glen would often call out, "Lisa, stop it!" or "Lisa, please quit breaking things. You're running us out of business." Later, when nothing happened for a day, and we began to be afraid all the excitement was over, Al called, "Lisa, where are you? Please break just one more beer mug. We've begun to get used to it now. We miss you."

It was obvious to many of us from the beginning that the bric-a-brac boogie we had to contend with had centered its attention on one person in the warehouse—Julio. He is a likable, well-meaning, and good-looking young man, living what one would think was a reasonably secure life. And yet, was he really? Perhaps Al and Glen weren't always the easiest bosses in the world to get along with. Certainly the reorganization of the shelves gave Julio a considerable amount of dissatisfaction right at the time the activity started in earnest. So Julio might understandably have had frustrations. Could these frustrations have unconsciously produced an accumulated force that could hurl the housewares about? A physical medium can cause objects to move in his presence. Perhaps Julio was an untrained, potential physical medium? It is also true that poltergeist activity centering around one might tend to unsettle him, and cause him to become somewhat disturbed in his behavior. Historically, this has been true in several cases.

There was a time when the action followed Julio so closely

that I was tempted to think that he was consciously playing tricks. I suspected from time to time that he *must* have found some way to rig up a gadget for throwing things that no one else could discover. How a young man like Julio could invent a device so sophisticated that magicians and psychical researchers and policemen could not detect it was beyond me. But I didn't see how it could be otherwise. Julio would stop at a shelf and immediately after he moved, before he was five feet away from it, something would drop. I would start for the spot the moment he left, and be unable to reach it before a beer mug would clatter to the floor or a Coke bottle would shatter.

"How in the *devil* does he do it?" I asked not only myself but also Brooks and other people I knew to be adept at professional trickery. They all replied, "There *is* no gadget that wouldn't be visible afterwards." Even those who suggested, as one newspaperman did, that mercury could make an object fall, had to admit that the little ball of mercury would then remain on the shelf to be observed when we rushed up after the incident.

Not satisfied, however, without personal experimentation, I found myself attempting such tricks as putting a piece of ice on the end of a knife and watching the knife fall when melting set it off balance—and noting the wet spot the ice left. I took a chipped ashtray, of which Tropication Arts now had an abundant supply, and tipped it against a piece of dry ice, observing the smoke the dry ice exuded and the way it burned my hands when I carried it, and the long time it took before it released the dish. I tried rubber bands, which would never disappear for me afterward. I got nowhere. How our invisible playmate must have been laughing at me, as he continued to produce his phenomena almost under my nose, or at least as soon as my back was turned.

Even Pratt, whose scientific objectivity made him very careful about showing any enthusiasm, now surprised me by chiding me for my lack of faith in my own previous conclusions. My newspaper background, as opposed to his laboratory discipline, allowed me to become sorrowfully concerned when suspecting the possibility of trickery, and highly pleased at each occurrence that seemed to be supernormal beyond any reasonable doubt. I chalked up the several occasions that happened when Julio was out of the room as evidence for his side.

One day when Julio and I were alone in the warehouse, objects

fell under conditions about as controlled as you are likely to get
in these cases. Officer Sackett had decided to try an experiment
and had wiped one of the amber glass beer mugs clean of finger-
prints and placed it as a decoy on the second shelf at the north
end of Tier Three. He then stretched a rope down the middle
of Aisle Three and said that no one was to go on the other side
of it into Aisle Four. Julio and I, then, were outside of this
roped-off area, at the front desk in the warehouse, talking. Just
at twelve o'clock I glanced around and realized that everyone
else had gone to lunch. I said, "There's nobody in here but us.
Now is the time for something to happen."

At that very second a pop was heard, and we discovered that
a shot glass had fallen into Aisle Three at the north end, just
inside the rope. It had not broken. We left it there without touching it and returned to the desk; but I had hardly sat down when
a loud crash sounded from the same area. It was a beer mug,
just outside the rope at the same end of the same aisle. We did
not recall that such a mug had been on a shelf near there, so I
crawled under the rope and checked to see if the decoy mug
was still in its original place and its original condition on the
opposite side of the shelves. It was, at that moment. By the time
I returned to the desk, it was in Aisle Four in a thousand small
pieces.

Since I had been talking to Julio and looking at him during
every one of these occurrences, I certainly knew that he had not
made any of them happen—not consciously, at least. Why, then,
should I doubt him on other occasions? Because sometimes those
who are the focal point of poltergeist activity do take it upon
themselves to cause something to happen when affairs get dull.
They seem to need the excitement to continue to revolve around
them, and so they do by conscious physical means what they have
previously unconsciously caused to happen. "Could Julio finally
have succumbed to this?" I wondered sometimes. "And if so, how
was he doing it?" Back to that old problem again. As you can
imagine, I was in a turmoil. So were others. Al said he woke
up early every morning and lay in bed trying to figure out what
was going on in his stockroom.

"I know I don't have a ghost of a chance to understand it,"
he told us one morning, "but still I make the effort."

"That's the spirit," replied Glen.

"Oh, no," I moaned. "The poltergeist is the only one allowed to make bad jokes around here."

We were all finally converted into genuine unadulterated "believers" on Monday and Tuesday, January 23 and 24, when the activity got so fast and furious that no human, unless he had been on roller skates, could have rigged up enough devices to trigger things so fast. There were eight or ten people at a time in the warehouse that day, watching incredulously as objects dashed about inside the building, while outdoors thunder crashed and lightning flashed and the rain poured down as if Nature had lost all sense of discretion.

Larry Wolfe, a salesman for National Cash Register Company and the brother of artist Pat Wolfe, had heard her talking about The Thing that was giving the business to the business where she worked. He wanted to see for himself. "Around 12:30 on Monday afternoon I was standing by the order desk in the back of the stockroom," he told me later. "I heard a glass crash behind me and found a jigger had been broken. In rapid succession after that a Coke bottle crashed to the floor. Then another shot glass hit in the middle aisle. Pat caught a glimpse of it in flight. And then a shot glass fell in the third aisle. Moments later another bottle broke in Aisle Four, and then one of those carved coconuts that look like an Indian head landed in Aisle Two. Almost immediately after that an old cowbell they used to keep on the back door for delivery men to ring clanged down in that last aisle that seemed to be the favorite playground."

Larry's conclusion about the whole experience? "I knew that something was happening in which humans were not involved."

About that time Al and Glen began to gather up some of the jewelry items and the beer mugs to take into the front office, where nothing had been broken up until then. "Why should we lose any more money on this than we have to?" Al said. As Ruth May walked up Aisle One she noticed a carton of eighteen zombie glasses—those highball tumblers in which the potent drink called a "zombie" is served. The painters had just finished decorating the glasses with palm trees and flamingos. Ruth said, "Glen, you'd better secure those or they'll jump off the shelf." Glen did just that, fixing the lid tightly on the box and pushing it as far back as possible. After watching him do this, Ruth left the room. But she returned ten minutes later on a run because of the violent crash she had heard. Yes, it was the carton of eighteen zombie glasses landing in Aisle Four!

Al, standing at the south end of Aisle Two and looking toward the north, heard the crash and observed that no one was anywhere near it; but he did not see anything fly by. "I was very curious about this," he told me. "I was looking right that way and didn't see a thing move."

This kind of wild activity kept up all day long. Wally Komorek can tell us more about it. This Summit, New Jersey, man was an Army buddy of Al's. When he takes a Florida vacation he stops in, and, he says, "I usually give Al a hand with the work. I have lots of time."

Wally had walked in that day, been told about the ghost in the stockroom, and politely laughed it off. Then he entered the vortex, ready to go to work. Once, he laid a wooden tray with about six items on it—little boxes of jewelry in dozen or two-dozen lots, packages of this and that, a few beer mugs—on the second shelf on the east side of Tier Three. Then he walked away for a few minutes. Before he returned, the tray was heard to land with a thud in the middle of Aisle Four. There were many boxes on the shelf, so it couldn't have been pushed across. It would have had to go around. Of course, as usual, nobody was near; but plenty of people were in the room.

What does Wally Komorek now say about his afternoon of work at Tropication Arts? He says, "Half the things I saw that day, and later when I was there, I was in a position to know that no human being could have done it." He adds, "I didn't believe it when I came here. But now I believe it!"

Because of a previous commitment, I had been away when most of the big things crashed that day, but I saw enough smaller activity to wear me out trying to keep up with it. Around 4:30 Monday afternoon I had walked down Aisle Two and a corner of a small drawer containing nails caught on my skirt. I don't know why it caught, because there is not a rough spot on the drawer, as several of us have since ascertained. As my skirt started to pull the drawer from its place, I asked for help to get loose, saying, "I don't want to be responsible for one of these catastrophes." Julio came and released me and pushed the drawer firmly back into place. Then, trying to redd up an area along the west wall to make room for a carton, he placed a square

electric fan fifteen by fifteen inches in size on the top shelf of
Aisle Four. He had barely turned away when, at 4:34 exactly,
the fan landed precipitously on the cement. I turned and looked
at it, then walked the few steps back to my post at the desk. At
4:35 I heard a clatter behind my back. Not three feet behind me,
spilling its nails all over Aisle Three, was the same little drawer
that had tagged me in Aisle Two a few minutes before!

Tuesday was just as bad a day, with so much occurring so
frequently that we were all highly impressed by the versatility
and vigor of our haunt. When a whole carton of twenty-four beer
mugs crashed, Al finally relented and allowed an exorcism ceremony to be performed. After working hours, José Díaz, a chubby-
faced Cuban medium who is Julio's father-in-law-to-be, and of
whose beliefs Julio is highly skeptical, arrived laden with fern
fronds, cactus leaves, and other substances of magical significance
to him. He twisted some of the fronds into circles and placed
them strategically, intertwined with the cactus, at either end of all
the piles of rubble in the aisles. He lay other fern fronds across
the ends of the tiers and on the shelves. In a storage area at
the south end of the warehouse, up over the little room where
Al's office is, he constructed an altar with a rubber alligator in the
middle of it. (This was done because when José had visited the
warehouse previously he had seen the entity he believed was causing the trouble. It had shown itself to him in the form of a
prehistoric monster—a dinosaur, he thought, or an alligator.)

Here and there throughout the storeroom, José then laid little
piles of toys, saying to the evil entity, "Look, these are for you
to play with. Leave everything else alone." Then he sprinkled salt
and spices about and burned incense and said prayers.

We did not have an opportunity to learn whether or not the
exorcism was successful in itself, for Julio, embarrassed, refused to
come to work the next day. Not one dish flew or carton tumbled
all day long. When he came in on Thursday, Julio seemed somewhat impressed by all the strange fetishes that we had allowed
to remain there to do their work. We told him nothing had happened the day before, and he began to believe that perhaps the
exorcism had been successful after all. He insisted that the symbols
be left where they were.

Poor Curt cussed every time he had to walk over all the trash
as he searched for his wares on the shelves. Bea and other artists

began pleading with Julio to allow Curt to sweep up the hoodoo-voodoo and let the poltergeist return. We soon began to realize that we all missed the fun and excitement. Since The Thing, whatever it was, had proved to be harmless to people—although the dickens with property—we had become used to it, and now we wanted it back. We were all conditioned to jumping at every sudden noise, anyway, no matter where we were, and so we might as well have the old significant crashes to react to. Of course, the fact that Al and Glen were out hundreds of dollars worth of property had to be considered, but somehow we were inclined to let them do the worrying about that.

Finally, by early afternoon, Julio relented and let all José Díaz's fetishes be swept away. Within an hour an ashtray smashed! We all cheered! Julio grinned to realize that we hadn't been deserted by our destructive, but tremendously entertaining, companion. And even Al beamed the next morning when he heard about the ashtray and the other things that had been broken during the latter part of Thursday afternoon after the poltergeist returned. Nobody complained when the activity continued for several days more, although fortunately it never again reached the peak of devastation hit on January 23 and 24. Poltergeists are like that; they usually achieve a climax of activity and then taper off again. And when they finally leave, they seldom return. But ours, as I have intimated, was more pertinacious than most. He is not to be got rid of so lightly.

As soon as the activity ceased at Tropication Arts, after almost a month of spine-chilling and yet somehow oddly enchanting days, there was the usual newspaper denouement by a flat-footed and fuzzy-minded detective. He insisted that he had solved the entire case of the spook in the stockroom by extracting from a "sick" youth employed there the confession that it had all been done with a network of threads, which had been cleverly manipulated when no one was looking. The boy had also, the world was informed, placed boxes on the edge of those shelves, and then jets going by overhead had knocked them off. Those sturdy shelves in that solidly constructed cement block building, from which hefty policemen had been unable to shake objects with all their effort! The jets must have been flying awfully low.

Well, that's the way poltergeist cases go. The police love to mark a case neatly closed, and so do the newspapers when there is nothing more in the way of front page excitement going on. But our invisible entertainer had other ideas, which forced the Miami papers to add another chapter recounting its further exploits. They may have to say much more about it in the future—who knows?

You see, this poltergeist followed the boy out of town. It being slightly expensive to maintain your own personal, poltergeist indefinitely, Al and Glen reluctantly decided to fire Julio. This gave Bill Roll an opportunity that all parapsychologists yearn for—the chance to give the focal point, or active ingredient, in a poltergeist case careful scrutiny at a time while the force is still "hot." And so the Psychical Research Foundation offered to pay Julio's plane fare and wages while he visited in Durham for observation and testing. The youth was very reluctant to go; but finally, after a great deal of cajoling and corralling, I managed to get him on a plane for Durham the next week. He remained two weeks; and as this is written the final reports are not in from the doctors and researchers who tested him, so we do not yet know all the results. We will look forward to the future publication of his responses to the many different types of examinations he was given: An EEG (electroencephalogram) in which electrodes were attached to different parts of his skull and readings were taken to determine if there were any abnormal brain wave patterns; psychiatric interview; intelligence test; Rorschach, where he was asked to interpret ink blots; TAT (or thematic apperception test), a series of pictures with which he was asked to construct a story from which the doctor would make certain inferences about his personality, fantasy, and imagination; and word association tests involving terms taken from incidents in the warehouse. (These latter three were done while Julio was hooked up to a polygraph, or lie detector.) He was also examined by an endocrinologist, to determine whether there were any glandular abnormalities, and was given the Minnesota Multiphasic Personality Inventory which included about 580 questions for which True or False answers were given.

It is known so far that when he was tested for psychokinesis, or mind over matter effects, the results were suggestive of his having definite power in this area. He also had some ESP tests; and one seance was held, during which Julio went into trance almost immediately—more or less confirming our suspicion that he is a latent medium.

During the time that he was being tested, Julio and Bill Roll were invited to visit the offices of a very prominent parapsychologist, who shall be nameless because he quite naturally would not wish to have his name involved in a case that was being investigated by other researchers. At a time when Julio was beginning to feel quite pressured because of the many procedures and frequent delays that were upsetting him, he was in a room with Roll and four young members of the parapsychologist's staff. As Julio was standing near a doorway, a vase fell from a table in the hall outside and broke on the floor!

Mr. Roll says, "There was no way in which the four young men and I could see how he could have caused the incident fraudulently." He didn't add, but I am at liberty to, that it is really very significant that an event similar to those in the warehouse should have occurred under the watchful eyes of five researchers in a place where the youth could have had no opportunity to rig anything up.

Roll's statement about this entire case to a Miami newspaper reporter who called him was: "It was the best chance I've ever had to observe the breakage and movement of objects by some unexplained force. It was much better than the Seaford case, which was the best chance I had to observe such phenomena prior to this time. In Miami I was able to observe with my own eyes numerous instances of movement of objects and check for the possibility of fraud or accident. Neither existed."

Now, if Julio still is able, by some peculiar force from his mind, unconsciously to cause objects to fall from shelves, we probably have not heard the last of him yet. I will keep a careful watch on him in the future places where he works. It might be that there will be other outbreaks of poltergeist activity from time to time, when the boy becomes dissatisfied with a job or with other conditions in his life. I am certain there are people who would be willing to pay for any damage that he might cause if this were to occur again, because a genuine poltergeist boy is such an interesting rarity that he should be cherished rather than scorned.

And so, as we watch and wait for another outburst of Miami's persistent poltergeist, this chapter cannot actually be considered completed. It, as well as the book itself, will have to end like an old-time serial—*To be continued.*

BIBLIOGRAPHY

Bardacke, Frances. "The Swinging World of 'Yankee Jim,'" *San Diego Magazine*, January 1966.

Beaglehole, Ernest. *Some Modern Hawaiians*, U. of Hawaii Research Pub. #19.

Bell, Charles Bailey, M.D. *The Bell Witch, A Mysterious Spirit.*

Bradshaw, Wesley. *The National Tribune*, December 1880.

Cogswell, Leander W. *History of the Town of Henniker, Merrimack Co., N.H.* Republican Press Assoc., 1880.

Cummings, Abraham. *Immortality Proved by the Testimony of Sense.* Bath: J. G. Torrey, 1826.

Dow, Joseph. *History of the Town of Hampton, N.H.* Salem, Mass. Press 1893.

Drake, Samuel Adams. *New England Legends and Folklore.* Boston: Little, Brown & Co., 1910.

Duncan, Wm. Cary. *The Amazing Madame Jumel.* New York: Frederick A. Stokes Co., 1935.

Fodor, Nandor. *On the Trail of the Poltergeist.* New York: Citadel Press, 1958.

Freeman, Douglas Southall. *R. E. Lee.* New York: Charles Scribner's Sons, 1934.

Holzer, Hans. *Yankee Ghosts.* Indianapolis: The Bobbs-Merrill Company, Inc., 1966.

Huntington, James Lincoln. *Forty Acres.* Hastings House, n.d.

Ingram, M. V. *Authenticated History of the Famous Bell Witch.* Clarksville, Tennessee: 1894.

Jones, Louis C. *Things that Go Bump in the Night.* New York: Hill & Wang, 1959.

Kamakau, Samuel M. *The People of Old*. Bishop Museum Press, 1964.

Kane, Harnett. *New Orleans Item,* August 8, 1933.

Lowndes, Marion. *Ghosts that Still Walk*. New York: Alfred A. Knopf, 1941.

Malo, David. *Hawaiian Antiquities*. Bishop Museum, 1951.

Parks, Lillian Rogers, and Leighton, Frances S. *My Thirty Years Backstairs in the White House*. Fleet Pub. Co., 1961.

Scherts, Helen Pitkin. *Legends of Louisiana*. New Orleans Journal, 1922.

Shelton, Wm. Henry. *The Jumel Mansion*. New York: Houghton Mifflin Co., 1916.

Westervelt, W. D. *Hawaiian Legends of Volcanoes*. Tokyo: Charles Tuttle Co., 1963.

———. *Legends of the Gods and Ghosts*. Boston: George H. Ellis Co., 1915.

Withington, Antoinette. "Ghostly Processions in Hawaii," *Harper's Monthly Magazine,* May 1937: 605–610.